OVERCOMING
EVIL IN THE LAST DAYS

OVERCOMING
EVIL IN THE LAST DAYS

RICK JOYNER

© Copyright 2003 — Rick Joyner

Destiny Image® **Publishers, Inc.**
P.O. Box 310
Shippensburg, PA 17257-0310

"Speaking to the Purposes of God for This Generation
and for the Generations to Come"

ISBN 0-7684-2178-0

For Worldwide Distribution
Printed in the U.S.A.

4 5 6 7 8 9 10 11 12 13 14 / 06 05 04 03

This book and all other Destiny Image, Revival Press, MercyPlace, Fresh Bread, Destiny Image Fiction, and Treasure House books are available at Christian bookstores and distributors worldwide.

For a U.S. bookstore nearest you, call **1-800-722-6774**.
For more information on foreign distributors, call **717-532-3040**.
Or reach us on the Internet:
www.destinyimage.com

CONTENTS

INTRODUCTION

SATAN'S CORD OF THREE STRANDS

In this book we will examine the three most powerful evil strongholds that together bind and control fallen mankind—racism, witchcraft, and the religious spirit. As Ecclesiastes 4:12 states, "And if one can overpower him who is alone, two can resist him. A cord of three strands is not quickly torn apart." These three, working together in a deadly alliance, can be seen at the root of almost all the death and destruction that has been the bane of human history. These are satan's cord of three strands that are very difficult to break when they work together. It is crucial for us to understand these strongholds because without this understanding we cannot comprehend the world in which we live, particularly the ultimate conflict between good and evil that will mark the end of this age.

I have previously addressed these strongholds in articles and have also written a series of booklets on spiritual strongholds. However, this book is a much more in-depth study. As we seek understanding of the ultimate evil forces, we must always keep in mind that it is the truth that sets us free. Our goal is to understand not just the evil, but even more so the counterforce of truth that alone can break the power of evil. Truth breaks the power of evil by displacing it. Our goal is not just to stop doing evil, but to do good, and to thereby bear fruit for the Kingdom of God.

As the Lord taught in Luke 11:24-26, when an unclean spirit goes out of a man it will try to return if the place it left is not occupied. Not only will it return, but it will also bring seven other evil spirits more powerful than itself. Therefore, our goal must always be to not only cast out the evil, but to fill the place it occupied with the truth of the Holy Spirit. The best way to do this is to drive out the evil and deception with the truth—the counterpower to the deception. We therefore are not just trying to reveal what is wrong, but to reveal God's righteousness and truth that will drive out the evil. We then want to sink our roots deeper and deeper into His truth so that it is not just a concept that we believe, but the nature of who we are.

It is for this reason that you will notice some redundancies in this study. Repetition is required for retention; thus the goal of this study is not just to illuminate the evil, but to drive the seed of truth deeper and deeper into our hearts so that it can never be lost or stolen. Just as a healthy tree has roots growing below the surface that are as extensive as the branches above it, we want to be within all that our outward actions reveal. We want truth in our innermost being. Then the fruit that we produce will not only be abundant, but be of the highest quality and strength.

As the Lord teaches in the parable of the sower, every seed of truth will be tested before it can bear fruit. Our goal is to not only pass the tests, but to bear much fruit. We do this by first getting free ourselves, and then by also setting others free of these evil strongholds. Christians are called to be the ultimate freedom fighters.

As we begin to understand each of the ultimate strongholds addressed in this book, we must also understand how they tend to work together. For example, if we start to experience freedom from racism or a control spirit, which is a form of witchcraft, the devil will usually send a religious spirit to encourage us to unrighteously judge others who are still bound by racism or the control spirit. In this way the religious spirit builds another stronghold, one of pride, that will make a way for the racism and control spirits to return. Then, when these strongholds are empowered by the religious spirit, they become much more powerful than before.

Because of these interrelationships and cross strategies of the enemy, it is important for us to study all of these together. We must also always keep in mind that we are not warring against flesh and blood, but against the evil forces that are controlling people. God gives His grace to the humble, and so we must endeavor to always walk in the humility of knowing that just because we have been given grace, it does not make us any better than those who do not yet have it. In fact, we are the servants of those who are not yet free, servant warriors who have been sent to set them free.

It is entirely understandable that confronting such issues is frightening to you. However, some foolishly think it is better to remain ignorant of such things and let others do the spiritual warfare thing—those who think this way are the ones who will inevitably fall to the worst snares of the devil. Truth is fundamental to Christianity, and if we are true followers of Christ, we will be in pursuit of truth regardless of the responsibilities that it brings upon us. It is our calling to rule and reign with Him, and our training for reigning is this life. The true Christian life is precisely all about growing in truth and using the divinely powerful weapons that we have been given to destroy the works of the devil.

If the Lord had wanted things to be easy for us He could have bound the devil immediately after His resurrection. We must understand that the battle we are engaged in is a good fight. There can be no victories without a battle. We have been entrusted with divinely powerful weapons that no evil can stand against. The Bible is God's plan, and if you have not done so yet, read the end of the story—we win! You are on the side that cannot lose. The battle is for our sake, so that we can grow in the character and faith which will decide the authority that we are entrusted with in the age to come.

The purpose of this book is to shine light into the darkness, which is the root of satan's power over mankind. Because the devil dwells in darkness, truth or illumination begins to break his power over our lives. One Christian who walks in truth can be the most powerful force on earth. One such Christian is the greatest terror in hell. That is what you are called to be. If you are walking in the light you will fear no evil, but all evil will be in fear of you. As we are promised in James 4:7, if we resist the devil he will not only leave us alone, he will *flee* from us. Far too many spend their Christian lives desperately trying to ward off the attacks of the enemy. It is time that we arise in the authority we have been given to put him on the defensive. That is your calling.

You have a promise in 1 Peter 5:6-10:

Humble yourselves, therefore, under the mighty hand of God, that He may exalt you at the proper time,

casting all your anxiety on Him, because He cares for you.

*Be of sober **spirit**, be on the alert. Your adversary, the devil, prowls around like a roaring lion, seeking someone to devour.*

*But resist him, firm in **your** faith, knowing that the same experiences of suffering are being accomplished by your brethren who are in the world.*

*And after you have suffered for a little while, the God of all grace, who called you to His eternal glory in Christ, will Himself perfect, confirm, strengthen **and** establish you.*

PART ONE

RACISM

CHAPTER ONE

THE ULTIMATE POWERS OF EVIL

WE FIRST ADDRESS THE STRONGHOLD OF RACISM because its power is rooted in two of the ultimate yokes that hold people in bondage, and therefore are the roots of the evil one's power. When they are broken it is much easier to be set free from every other yoke of bondage.

Racism is one of the ultimate strongholds that binds mankind, and is the primary stronghold that empowers the spirit of death. It is the linchpin yoke of bondage that empowers what I call "satan's cord of three strands." For this reason he seeks to impose it on every church and movement that is making a spiritual advance. It has been an effective strategy as most in history have fallen to this great evil in at least one of its forms. Because deception *is* deceptive, those who are bound by it often believe they are the most free from the prejudices of racism.

You may think I am carrying this problem a bit too far, but both the Scriptures and history confirm it. First we must understand that racism is not just about race. We must also understand how racism is rooted in two of the most basic evil powers that have controlled mankind since the fall—fear and pride. A person becomes a racist either because of pride in the flesh, or fear of those who are different, both of which are a thick veil over the human soul. Racism is one of the most powerful of the evil world rulers.

THE SIGN

The harvest will come at the end of the age, and will be the reaping of everything that has been sown in man, both the good and the evil. Both fear and pride will come to full maturity in man at the end. When Jesus was asked about the signs that would accompany the end of the age He said, "...nation will rise against nation, and kingdom against kingdom..." (Mt. 24:7). The word that is translated "nation" in this text is the Greek word *ethnos*, from which we derive our English word "ethnic." This makes clear that a prominent sign at the end of this age and His return will be ethnic conflict. In fulfillment of this Scripture, one of the greatest issues now facing the world and the Church is ethnic conflict.

The world is losing control of its racial problems. The cause is a spiritual power that no legislation or human agency can stop. Only that which is bound in Heaven can be bound upon the earth. If the Church does not face this problem—overcoming the racism within our own ranks so that we can take spiritual authority over it—the world will soon fall into an abyss of chaos, destruction, and suffering of unprecedented proportions—all because of racial conflict. As the Lord stated in His discourse about the end as recorded in Luke 21:25-26:

> *And there will be signs in sun and moon and stars, and up on the earth dismay among nations* [ethnos], *in perplexity at the roaring of the sea and the waves,*

men fainting from fear and the expectation of the things which are coming upon the world; for the powers of the heavens will be shaken.

We read in Revelation 17:15, "...The waters which you saw...are peoples and multitudes and nations and tongues." In the text from Luke, we see that the "roaring of the sea and the waves" is the result of the turmoil among the *ethnos,* or ethnic conflicts. This will become so great that men will faint from the fear of it.

This problem will not go away with time, but will increase. The longer we wait to confront this stronghold, the more powerful it will become. Pressure is now building in almost every world-class city, but when it erupts it will not be confined to only the cities. It is rising up between cultures and nations, with pressure building to the boiling point. Ancient cultural wounds and offenses are motivating the politics of many nations. We can point to almost every single war and conflict in the world today as being rooted in racism of some form.

Racism is like fuel that has been poured over the dry tinder of the world—the only thing it lacks in any place is the striking of a match to ignite it. The frenzy of the fire of racism can be unprecedented in releasing demented human passions. After the recent murders of nearly one million people in Rwanda over the period of a few weeks, some of those who were the most involved in the slaughter of thousands of people said that they did not even remember doing it. They were not denying their guilt as they sat covered in blood, but explained that it was like something came over them and they were just carried along by it. They are right.

What happened in Rwanda was one of satan's dress rehearsals for what he wants to release on the earth. If we are arrogant enough to believe that we live in a country too civilized for such a thing to happen, that very pride could be the only door that the devil needs. Of all the nations in Africa, Rwanda was the one where such a thing was the least expected to happen. Ninety percent Christian, the Rwandans were considered the most peaceful, loving people in Africa. Nazi Germany was also considered a Christian nation. How did the devil take them over? This is a question we must answer.

The Higher Power

The Lord has demonstrated His power to calm the storm and the sea. King David declared of Him, "By awesome deeds Thou dost answer us in righteousness, O God of our salvation,... Who dost still the roaring of the seas, the roaring of their waves, and the tumult of the peoples" (Ps. 65:5,7).

The Lord will again stand up and calm the roaring sea with His Word. The Lord came to destroy the works of the devil, and He has sent us with this same purpose. We are not here as spectators to watch, but to stand against the darkness, and to push it back. We must, however, know our enemy—racism is one of the ultimate enemies of the truth, the gospel, and mankind. It is an enemy that we must face in the Church. It is an enemy that we will conquer.

Racism is not just a demon, or even a principality—it is a "world ruler." It is one of the most powerful strongholds on the earth, and it has sown more death and destruction than any other. The most deadly wars in history, including World War II, were ignited by racism. This powerful spirit prepares the way for and empowers the spirit of death. The apostle Paul understood that when the ultimate racial barrier is overcome, the division between Jew and Gentile, as they are grafted together in Christ, will mean nothing less than "life from the dead" (Rom. 11:15), or the overcoming of death.

THE ROOTS OF RACISM

As stated, there are two foundations of racism. The first is pride, in one of its most base forms—pride in the flesh. It is judging others by the externals, which is the ultimate form of pride. In its basic form, pride is simply the statement that we feel sufficient within ourselves, that we do not really need God or anyone else. This creates an obvious barrier between ourselves and others.

The second foundation of racism is fear. Insecurity is a result of the fall and the separation between God and man. The insecure are afraid of those who are different and those they cannot control. Racism is a powerful and deeply interwoven combination of both pride and fear.

Fear breaks relationships just as trust is the bridge that establishes relationships. You can have love and even genuine forgiveness, but if you do not have trust, a relationship is not possible. Fear and pride tear down the trust that make a relationship possible, therefore creating division.

BREAKING THE POWER OF EVIL

The cross of Christ confronts and overcomes both the pride of man and his insecurity. The Holy Spirit was sent to convict the world of sin because it is the revelation of our sin that drives us to the cross to find grace and forgiveness. This destroys our pride and establishes our dependency on the Savior, which also restores our trust in Him. The deeper the cross works in us, the more humble we will become, and the more secure in His love. When we, who are so foreign to God's nature, are accepted back into Him by His grace, it works a tolerance in us for those who are different from our nature. Subsequently, those who become spiritual begin to judge from a spiritual perspective, not after the flesh.

Therefore from now on we recognize no man according to the flesh; even though we have known Christ according to the flesh, yet now we know Him thus no longer.

Therefore if any man is in Christ, he is a new creature; the old things passed away; behold, new things have come.

2 Corinthians 5:16-17

Most especially, the Church should not judge others according to the color of their skin or their cultural background. We must learn to see by the Spirit and judge only by the Spirit, just as it was said of Jesus:

The Spirit of the Lord will rest on Him, the spirit of wisdom and understanding, the spirit of counsel and strength, the spirit of knowledge and the fear of the Lord.

And He will delight in the fear of the Lord, and He will not judge by what His eyes see, nor make a decision by what His ears hear.

Isaiah 11:2-3

If we are going to walk as He walked, we too, must learn to see and hear as He did. This is the great lesson of the two men on the road to Emmaus. The resurrected Christ appeared to these disciples and preached to them about Himself for quite awhile. This was Christ preaching Christ—it will never be more anointed than that! Yet they still could not recognize Him. Why? Because "...He appeared in a different form..." (Mk. 16:12).

One of the primary reasons we miss the Lord when He tries to draw near to us is because we tend to know even the Lord after a form rather than by the Spirit. If we are Charismatics, we tend to only recognize Him when He comes to us through a Charismatic. Or if we are a Baptist, we tend to only know Him when He comes to us through a Baptist. However, He will usually approach us in a form that is different than what we are used to. He did so with His own disciples after His resurrection. This is because He is always seeking to have us know Him after the Spirit, not through externals.

The Lord declared: "For I say to you, from now on you will not see Me until you say, 'Blessed is He who comes in the name of the Lord!' " (Mt. 23:39) We will not see Him until we learn to bless those whom He sends to us, regardless of the form in which they come. Even Israel did not recognize the Lord when He came to them in a form that they were not expecting. This is not a new problem with God's people, but it remains a serious one.

THE GLORY OF DIVERSITY

The Church is called to have, and to be a reflection of, the answers to the most fundamental human problems. Racism is one of the most basic and deadly problems in human history, and its power is increasing greatly at this time. However, the Lord declared: "My house shall be called a house of prayer for all the nations [ethnos]..." (Mk. 11:17). The Church has not fulfilled her destiny until she truly becomes a house of prayer for all ethnic peoples. This makes the Church the ultimate antithesis to the evil of racism.

Paul said, "tongues are for a sign" (1 Cor. 14:22). What sign? The sign that the Church is to be the antithesis to the tower of Babel, where men's languages were scattered, and where men were separated into different races and cultures. We see the first great demonstration of this on the Day of Pentecost, at the very birth of the Church.

Now there were Jews living in Jerusalem, devout men from every nation [ethnos] under heaven.

And when this sound occurred, the crowd came together, and were bewildered, because they were each one hearing them speak in his own language.

Acts 2:5-6

The Church is the place where men will be unified again, regardless of race, culture, language, etc. Is it not interesting that Jews from every *ethnos* heard and understood in one language? Jesus is the Word of God, or God's communication to us. When men see His glory, when He is lifted up, all men will be drawn to Him and will understand with one heart again. The Church that truly worships Him will be a demonstration of that. Paul told the Galatians that in the Church every convert, from any cultural background or sex, has an equal standing before God.

For all of you who were baptized into Christ have clothed yourselves with Christ.

There is neither Jew nor Greek, there is neither slave nor free man, there is neither male nor female; for you are all one in Christ Jesus.

Galatians 3:27-28

There may be differences in our standing before God in such things as governmental authority, or within a specific ministry, but that has nothing to do with race, sex, or cultural background. Even the newest born-again Christian can go as boldly before the throne of God as the greatest preacher in the world. God does not show partiality, and if we are walking by His Spirit, neither will we.

This is just the beginning of our study of this ultimate enemy of the Church and mankind. Before we proceed, I ask you to stop and ask the Lord if there are any roots of this evil in your own heart; and if there are, ask Him to help you see them and repent of them.

The gates of hell are the enemy's access points into our life, and racism is one of the biggest doors the evil one now has into the world, and into our own individual lives. Therefore, those who escape the shackles of racism become some of the greatest threats to the power of the evil one in this world and who truly possess the power to shut the gates of hell. To be free of racism is to have replaced fear and pride with humility and faith, two of the greatest powers on earth. That is our goal in this study. Now we will go on to examine the major tentacles of racism's power and control.

Chapter Two

The Tyranny
of the Familiar

The psychological problem called "the tyranny of the familiar" is considered by many to be one of the most difficult to understand. It is a powerful yoke that can crush the potential and personality of human beings. It is one of the strongest spiritual yokes that binds fallen human beings and the Church. This yoke has baffled psychologists but it has baffled Christian leaders for even longer, sometimes turning new Christians into "old wineskins" in a matter of weeks, making them too rigid and inflexible to receive new truth.

Likewise, psychologists cannot understand why a high percentage of girls who grow up in the home of an alcoholic father, regardless of the pain and torment that this caused, will almost invariably marry a heavy drinker. Why do abused women risk their lives to protect their abusers? Great cultures, such as Germany was before World War II, will expend themselves and even perish following demented leaders. As incomprehensible as it seems, the familiar, although painful and dangerous, is still more desirable to them than the unfamiliar regardless of the fact that it offers much more hope.

This is the same yoke that keeps many ethnic groups from breaking out of their sociological and economic barriers. In spite of all the talk and genuine frustrations, most are afraid of change. Why is it that we so easily come into bondage to the familiar? *Basically it is because we tend to put our security in our environment instead of in the Lord.*

To institute true change, a strong trust must be built as a bridge out of our situation. This usually takes more time and effort than most people are willing to sacrifice. This is not a new problem. We even see this bondage in the children of Israel when they preferred the flesh pots of Egypt over the supernatural provision of God. Jeremiah 48:11-12 also addresses this issue in relation to the nation of Moab.

> *"Moab has been at ease since his youth; he has also been undisturbed on his lees, neither has he been emptied from vessel to vessel, nor has he gone into exile. Therefore he retains his flavor, and his aroma has not changed.*
>
> *"Therefore behold, the days are coming," declares the Lord, "when I shall send to him those who tip vessels, and they will tip him over, and they will empty his vessels and shatter his jars."*

The Lord was talking about change when describing being emptied from vessel to vessel. This was how wine was purified in those times. It was poured into a vessel and allowed to sit for a time. As it sat the impurities would settle to the bottom. Then it was poured into another vessel and allowed to sit so that the remaining impurities could again settle. Therefore, the more the wine had been emptied from vessel to vessel, the more pure it became. Because Moab had not been subjected to the purifying changes, the "wine" of that nation was impure; therefore, the Lord vowed to pour it out.

Every time the wine was poured into a new vessel it was unsettled—there was commotion and stirring which would bring the impurities to the surface. Whenever we are thrust into change, many things will begin to surface in our lives. This is a reason why the Lord often allows radical changes to impact our lives, which are almost always disconcerting. Usually we will see very quickly just how much we have trusted in the "vessel" we occupy, instead of the Lord. But we will settle down again, and we will be more pure. Change is cleansing. That is one reason why the Lord kept Israel moving most of the time in the wilderness.

THE WINE OF AMERICA

Now let us look at how this applies in a national situation. A good example is found as we look at the problems of the black race in America. Crime and violence in the inner cities can usually be traced to family problems. Unfortunately, a low percentage of black families have a father at home, and many of those who are at home are poor role models. Of course, some of the great fathers in America are also black, but in general, there is a serious problem in the majority of black families that can be traced to the lack of a strong father. What is the root of this problem? In one word—slavery.

Think about what the fathers in slave families had to go through. It is difficult to comprehend what it was like for a father to go to sleep each night knowing that he could be sold the next day and never see his family again. His wife, children, or both, could be sold, and he would never even know where they went. What would that do to the family? Fathers, mothers, and children alike could not really give their hearts to each other because of the terrible pain that they would inevitably suffer. The tearing apart of these families became the root of some of the great social problems in America today. It is a social wound that must be addressed and healed, or we will pay an increasingly high price until it is much more than we can afford.

THE DIABOLICAL ROOT

In 1712, a slave owner in the West Indies named Wilson Lynch wrote a letter to the British colonies in Virginia devising a strategy to break up slave families and loyalties thus keeping them from rising in rebellion. He projected that when the black family loyalties were destroyed, the only loyalty that the slaves would hold would be to their owner. Lynch also declared that when this strategy was implemented, it would destroy the fabric of black families for several hundred years. Of course this was a letter from hell, and the diabolical prophecy came true. Black women have had to be both father and mother to their families for centuries, and they are having a difficult time accepting fathers in their rightful place. Fathers are having just as hard a time taking their place.

Those who face this problem and overcome it are able to become some of the greatest fathers of all; and black families who are united are arising to become some of the great and noble families. This is why the television series *Roots* had such a powerful impact on America. It addressed the core problem like few movies, books, or art ever have, and called a great and noble people to find their roots in their families again.

If the white race, or any other people, had suffered the same historic problems as the black race, we would be having the same problems they are having now, and maybe worse.

However, I have heard many white leaders unbelievably say we would have no inner city problems if blacks just had some ambition. What impact do they think the drudgery, toil, and oppression of slavery had on the work ethic? Such deep cultural wounds cannot be healed without the intervention of the cross.

The black race in America was subjected to slavery for the same reason that the Lord allowed Israel to become slaves in Egypt—they have a destiny with God. When they come into this destiny, the rest of America is going to be very thankful for this great, noble, and free people in our midst. It is the destiny of the black race to carry freedom to a new level. This will be true freedom, with the dignity and honor that God created men to have.

THE POWER FOR HEALING

We know it is by the Lord's stripes that we are healed and receive the authority for healing in the very place where we are wounded. The black race is going to embrace the cross, receive healing for their own wounds, and start loving white Americans with such a power that we will all be set free by that love. The Uncle Tom of *Uncle Tom's Cabin* truly was a prophetic figure. Uncle Tom is understandably offensive to black Americans who have not yet been to the cross, but he is a type of Christ to those who have. In spite of all the abuse that he suffered at the hands of his owners, he was more free than they were and he was willing to use his great freedom to lay down his own life to bring about his owner's salvation. When the black believers in America have been fully healed, they will bring revival and true spiritual liberty to the whole nation, even, and especially to their oppressors.

The inner cities of America will ultimately become the inner sanctuary of God's tabernacle—the place where His glory and presence dwells. The greatest move of God that America has yet to experience will come out of the inner cities. The suburban church may have the gold, but the inner-city church will make them jealous with the glory. Those who are wise will take the gold they have and use it to build a tabernacle for the Lord that is not made with hands, but with people.

THE NATIONAL CALL

America is made up of every other nation, which is the foundation of the greatness that has been obtained, but it is also the foundation of our greatest problems. Even so, we have the potential to touch something of the glory of God that few other nations have. Our nation has the setting of another great Pentecost, which was a place where men came to dwell "from every nation under heaven" (Acts 2:5). We actually have the greatest opportunity to overcome and demonstrate the solution to one of the world's most deadly problems. When our great day comes we must also be as those of the first Pentecost, in which the Church was "all with one accord" (Acts 2:1 KJV), or in unity.

America is at the threshold of either her greatest victory or greatest failure. This powerful last-day stronghold will either be defeated on our shores, or it will defeat us. America will rise to even greater heights as a nation and world leader, or she will fall like every previous great world power. If we do not embrace this glorious potential, we will be destroyed by the problems.

When the Lord described the judgment, He said He was going to separate the nations into "sheep" and "goats" (see Mt. 25:31-46). The sheep will inherit His kingdom, and the goats eternal punishment. He said they would be distinguished by these characteristics; the sheep were those who, when He was thirsty, gave Him water; when He was hungry, gave Him food;

and when He was a stranger they took Him in (see v. 35). When the sheep inquired when they did this, He answered: "...Truly I say to you, to the extent that you did it to one of these brothers of Mine, even the least of them, you did it to Me" (v. 40).

One of the primary issues on which we will be judged will be our oneness with those who are different from us. Even the nations will be separated in this way. We know that at the end many nations will have gone to a terrible destruction, but we also know that some of the kingdoms of this world will have become the kingdoms of our Lord (see Rev. 11:15). The nations that will be judged to be "sheep," so as to enter His Kingdom, will be those who are open to foreigners and strangers.

This is a fundamental issue on which we will all be judged, and it is a reason why the Lord has bestowed His blessings upon America, and a number of other nations, to the degree that He has. Because racism deals with two of the most basic issues of the human heart—fear and pride—confronting these issues is one of the greatest opportunities that we have for entering His Kingdom.

Humility is a basic characteristic that enables us to be open to those who are different from us. It also helps others to lower their defenses against us. Because God "gives grace to the humble" (see Jas. 4:6), overcoming this problem opens us up like nothing else to the grace of God. When we add Christian love to this and become devoted to building up one another rather than tearing each other down, we are building upon the foundation of the Kingdom.

CHAPTER THREE

HEALING
CULTURAL WOUNDS

CULTURAL SINS ARE PASSED DOWN from
generation to generation until men recognize them, humble
themselves, and repent for the sins of their fathers. This prayer
of repentance so often seen in the Old Testament was usually
prayed by the most righteous men, like Daniel, who had
nothing to do with the sin. They simply understood this
principle and were willing to stand in the gap for their people.
This was the foundation of the cross and is the true nature of
Christ and those who would be Christlike.

Biblical repentance is more than just saying we are sorry,
or even feeling sorry—it is turning from our evil ways. The
white church in the South was one of the bastions that gave
birth to demented theologies and philosophies that justified
and perpetuated slavery. The Southern Baptist Convention was
actually born in an attempt to justify and perpetuate the
institution of slavery. Even though the Southern Baptist
Convention of today is quite different from the original

convention, and it is important to note that there have been many Southern Baptists on the very forefront of the war against racism, there is a reason why eleven o'clock on Sunday morning is still the most segregated hour of the week. There are still bastions of racism in the Southern Baptist Convention and most other denominations and movements within the Church.

This is not meant to point the finger at any single group. The whole Church is one of the bastions of this most powerful stronghold of the enemy—racism. That is one main reason why we have so many denominations. However, the Church will someday be free, and Southern Baptists will help to lead us out of this terrible darkness that is now sweeping the earth. The Southern Baptists are on the verge of a great revival and it will be ignited by their unyielding assault on this terrible evil power of racism.

The white Southern Baptist Church should have had the honor of doing what Martin Luther King, Jr. did—taking the leadership in this great battle against the world ruler of racism. Even so, the Southern Baptist Church will take up the fight, and will ultimately lead it. The Lord delights in redemption—it is His primary business. He will delight in taking what was meant for evil in the Southern Baptist Convention and using it for good, destroying the very evil that tried to use His Church this way.

THE LIGHT OF THE CHURCH

Racism is one of the world's most serious problems, and the Church must show the world the answer to this problem. However, we will not have spiritual authority over the world's problems if we have the same strongholds within ourselves. We must recognize that the Church today is still one of the most powerful bastions of racism, and it is still one of the most segregated institutions in the world. There are some notable exceptions to this, but generally the presence of racism in the Church is very real.

Spiritual bigotry is just as prevalent as the natural form. Spiritual racism is at work when we judge other churches, movements, or people as inferior or to be feared, because they are not a part of our group. This spiritual form of racism is a root cause of many of the present divisions and denominations in the body of Christ.

When Paul listed the qualifications for elders in the Church, he specified that they must be "hospitable" (see Tit. 1:8). In the original Greek this Scripture actually states, "one who shows hospitality to aliens or foreigners." Basically he was saying that to be a leader of the Church, a believer had to be open to those who were different. This is fundamental to true spiritual leadership. One who cannot value those who are different is either too proud or too insecure to be in Church leadership.

THE NATURE OF OUR UNITY

While the whole world is degenerating into increasing chaos from its ethnic conflicts, the Church will become increasingly unified. However, we must understand our unity. This does not mean that we all become the same, or submit to the same organizational structure, just as a husband can never become one with his wife by trying to make her a man. Our unity is based on the *recognition* and *appreciation* of our differences.

The whole creation reflects the Lord's love for diversity. He makes every snowflake, every tree, and every person different. He also desires to make every church *different*. These differences, however, are not designed to create conflict but to complement one another. It is only because of our continued distance from the Lord, and the resulting insecurity, that we view these differences as threats.

I am not implying that there will be no doctrinal and procedural differences in conflict between churches and movements. We must also understand that the true unity of the Church will not come by compromising our convictions. Even so, most of the differences that have brought conflict and division in the Church are not serious enough for us to divide over. In many cases, those whom we resist the most are the very ones we need the most to give *proper* balance and perspective to our vision of the truth.

During my 20 plus years in the Church, I have never witnessed a single division that was really based on a genuine commitment to truth. Men may have used doctrine or procedure as an excuse to divide from each other, but the real reason behind every split that I have witnessed was territorial preservation. This is a most deadly and selfish evil in the Church and a major foundation of our spiritual racism.

As stated, racism empowers the spirit of death, and this spirit has probably killed more churches and movements than any other enemy. Until we are free of this enemy, we will not have spiritual authority over it in human affairs. The only answer for us and the world is the cross. At the cross the dividing walls are taken down and we are free to come into true unity.

Another of the most significant barriers in the world today is the barrier between men and women. This is also related to racism. It is also true that one of the enemy's primary strategies against humanity is to blur the distinctions between men and women. Why would he do this if he is trying to divide us? Simply, because I cannot become one with my wife by making her into a man. Neither can a man become the true man that he was created to be until he learns to properly relate to women, recognizing and appreciating their differences.

Men will be unable to have a true perception of the world or anything else, including the Lord, until they are open to the woman's perspective about these things. The same is true for women. We must take our different perspectives and put them together if we are to see and understand clearly. Therefore, to walk in truth, we need each other. A woman will never be the lady that she has been created to be without learning to relate to men properly. There are deep wounds remaining on the part of each, but there is healing for all of them at the cross. There is no true healing anywhere else.

Likewise, no Charismatic, Pentecostal, Baptist, Methodist, or any other denomination will fulfill their own destiny without a proper relationship to the rest of the body of Christ. Even though the high priest of Israel was from the Tribe of Levi, he carried the stones that represented all the different tribes on his chest. This was to symbolize that those who walked in the high calling must carry all of God's people on their hearts.

Only when we have been delivered from our own spiritual/ethnic conflicts will we be called "a house of prayer for all nations" (Is. 56:7 NKJV), which is our fundamental calling. The times are about to press us into the desperation that is obviously required for us to do this. Let us not waste a day, for those who do not overcome the world will be overcome by it. When we begin to carry the cross, there is no spirit in this world that will not be subject to us. The cross has overcome the world, and when we embrace it, we too, will overcome the world.

There will never be true unity until we can see each other with the Lord's eyes, hear each other with His ears, and love each other with His heart. Every human problem in the world is impossible for men to overcome until they embrace the cross. But how can we expect men to do this until the Church does? We can only bear true spiritual fruit to the degree that we are abiding in the Vine. The stronger our union is with Him, the more fruit we will bear.

The Lord Jesus did not judge by what He saw with His natural eyes, or heard with His natural ears. His judgment was determined by what the Father revealed to Him. We cannot expect to walk in truth if we continue to receive our discernment from the secular press, the evening news, or even what we see with our own eyes at times. There is always a story behind the story that only God knows, which He will reveal to us if we turn to Him for our understanding.

As we have repeated often, we know that the Lord resists the proud but gives His grace to the humble. One of the most sure signs of true humility is being teachable; and a sign of ultimate humility is our willingness to be taught by someone who is different from us. This is why racial differences present one of the most potent opportunities for both the Lord and the devil. The devil uses it to create further division by releasing pride and fear. The Lord's purpose is always for us to grow in humility, faith, and love. Which will it be for us?

CHAPTER FOUR

A PRACTICAL STRATEGY

IN DEUTERONOMY 10:18-19, the Israelites were commanded to love the alien who was in their midst. In Deuteronomy 31:12, they were commanded to teach the alien. There is a great revelation in these Scriptures—*we must love someone before we can teach them.* Again, true spiritual authority is founded upon love.

America is the most powerful nation on earth at this time. An unbiased student of history would almost certainly consider it also the greatest and most benevolent power in history. What other nation would rebuild and restore its enemies the way that America did after World War II? What nation is ever on the scene of a crisis or natural disaster anywhere in the world before Americans? America is the most respected and emulated nation on earth. At the same time, it is also probably the most despised nation on earth. Why?

This hatred of America is not simply out of jealousy, but there is another basis to this hatred. Although it may be almost entirely unintentional, we continually offend and insult other cultures, sometimes even with our benevolence. Because we are a nation that is truly made up of those from every other nation, we should most certainly be the last to do this.

At last count almost sixty prime ministers and leaders of other nations have been educated in the United States, and yet a high percentage of these were anti-American in their policy. The Japanese military leader who planned the attack on Pearl Harbor, and the admiral who commanded the attack force, were both educated at Harvard University! When they came to America, one of their goals was to make American friends, but they were shunned by the American students. How could history have been changed if we had treated these men differently?

Between 200,000 and 300,000 foreigners are presently being educated in the United States. These students are usually the "cream of the crop" of their nations. Many are from nations where it is against the law to preach the gospel. We can reach the world without ever leaving home, just by showing hospitality to the foreigners who are presently on our college campuses. They are usually isolated and lonely. Many of them have nowhere to go during holidays. Because of these circumstances, their time in the United States is a negative experience. Many of them will one day be the leaders of their nations—some even prime ministers or foreign ministers. If churches that are located near campuses would just reach out to these foreigners, the world could be greatly impacted.

The Ultimate Racist Barrier

The ultimate racist barrier, with regard to spiritual power, is the barrier between Jew and Gentile. This separation is by God's design. The Jew is the natural seed of Abraham, and the Church is the spiritual seed. Together they are meant to represent the heavens and the earth, which is why the promise to Abraham was that his seed would be as "...the stars of the heavens, and as the sand which is on the seashore..." (Gen. 22:17). When the barrier between Jew and Gentile is overcome, it will signal the overcoming of the gulf between the spiritual and earthly realm, so that God, who is Spirit, may establish His eternal habitation with man.

The Jew is the embodiment of the humanistic spirit. They are a barometer of humanity—embattled within and without. As Paul said, "From the standpoint of the gospel they are enemies for your sake..." (Rom. 11:28). They were hardened, or made hard to reach, *for the sake of the gospel.* That is, the Jew represents the "acid test" of our message. Until we have a gospel that will make the Jew jealous, we do not really have it right. This means not only having it right doctrinally, but practically in the way that it changes us and that we reflect it in our preaching of the gospel. Perhaps this is why we are exhorted to preach the gospel to the Jew first, because when we preach to the Jew, we will quickly find out the quality of our message.

The wounds that have been afflicted upon Jews by the Church are some of the deepest and most tragic in history, which makes our job to reach them much more difficult. It will take an unprecedented humility on the part of the Church, which will enable the Lord to extend His unprecedented grace to trust us with an unprecedented anointing to reach the Jews. This is precisely God's plan. We cannot fulfill our commission as the Church without the Jews. They must be grafted back into God's Kingdom, which will require an unprecedented anointing, but first the Church has to be in a place of such humility and grace that every racist barrier in us is overcome. That is

41

why Paul confidently affirmed that when this happened, it would release the ultimate grace on mankind: "For if their rejection be the reconciliation of the world, what will their acceptance be but life from the dead?" (Rom. 11:15) The spirit of death and the racism that empowers it will be overcome when the Jew and Gentile have been grafted into the Vine together. Therefore, the Church must place the overcoming of racist barriers as a top priority. What can we do to build the bridges of trust between us?

The New Creation

The time period in which the Lord dealt almost exclusively with the Jews was about 2,000 years. The time of the Gentiles has now been about 2,000 years. What we are coming into now is the time of the Jew and the Gentile grafted into one new creation through Christ.

True unity is found in diversity, not in conformity. Converted Israel will not be like the Church. The Church is very far from being what God created her to be, and so is Israel. When they are truly joined together neither will be as they are now. We desperately need what the born-again Jew will bring into the Church. This does not imply a returning to the Law; rather the Church has not yet demonstrated on earth what the true new creation is. This union of the natural and spiritual seed of Abraham is required before it can be seen. This is the best wine, which the Lord has saved for last.

Many in the Church have embraced a "replacement theology," which replaces all of the present purposes of God for Israel with the Church. Others have embraced a "replacement, replacement theology" which replaces the Church with Israel. Both cloud the ultimate purpose for Israel and the Church. In the Book of Romans, which is the most explicit Book of New Covenant theology in the Scriptures, Paul clearly established God's purpose for each. He also warned against becoming "...arrogant toward the [natural] branches..." (Rom. 11:18), adding, "...Do not be conceited, but fear; for if God did not spare the natural branches, neither will He spare you" (Rom. 11:20-21). This is an issue of such importance that it can cut us off from God's purpose.

This does not imply that we must accept everything that Israel does. It is also clearly unbiblical that the Jews can be grafted into the purpose of God in any way except through Christ. But speaking of the natural branches, Paul declared: "I say then, God has not rejected His people, has He? May it never be!..." (Rom. 11:1) For God to reject natural Israel would be to impugn the very integrity of His promises made to Abraham and throughout the entire Old Testament, most of which there is no way to attribute to anyone but the natural Jew. Paul asserted:

> *Then what advantage has the Jew? Or what is the benefit of circumcision?*
>
> *Great in every respect. First of all, that they were entrusted with the oracles of God.*
>
> *What then? If some did not believe, their unbelief will not nullify the faithfulness of God, will it?*
>
> *May it never be! Rather, let God be found true, though every man be found a liar, as it is written, "that thou mightest be justified in Thy words, and mightest prevail when Thou art judged."*
>
> Romans 3:1-4
>
> *...from the standpoint of **God's** choice they are beloved for the sake of the fathers;*

for the gifts and the calling of God are irrevocable.

For just as you once were disobedient to God, but now have been shown mercy because of their disobedience,

so these also now have been disobedient, in order that because of the mercy shown to you they also may now be shown mercy.

For God has shut up all in disobedience that He might show mercy to all.

Romans 11:28-32

It will take extraordinary humility for the Church to fully see God's purpose in natural Israel, and it will take the same degree of humility for natural Israel to see God's purpose in the Church. But it will happen; and when it does, it will release an unprecedented measure of God's grace to both.

PAUL TO THE GENTILES AND PETER TO THE JEWS

Many believe that only converted Jews will be able to reach the Jews. This is contrary to His purpose, as well as the biblical testimony of how God reaches people. This was the reason the Lord sent Peter to the Jews and Paul to the Gentiles. According to our modern mentality, the Lord made a mistake. Certainly in our minds Paul, the Pharisee of Pharisees, would have been better able to relate to the Jews; and Peter, the simple fisherman, would obviously have been better able to reach the Gentiles. In the natural this is true, but our gospel is not natural; it is spiritual, and the natural mind still cannot comprehend it.

The Lord sent Paul to the Gentiles because he was an offense to them. Therefore, the only way that Paul could fulfill his commission was to be utterly dependent on the Holy Spirit— which is the only way the gospel is truly empowered. Likewise, the only way that Peter could reach the Jews was to be utterly dependent on the Holy Spirit. This is true of us all! Natural affinities do not help the gospel; they usually get in the way. "That which is born of the flesh is flesh, and that which is born of the Spirit is spirit" (Jn. 3:6).

Just as the Lord humbled the Gentiles by sending them Jews, He will humble the Jews by sending them Gentiles. Of course a few Jews will have some success in reaching their own people, but generally this will not be the way they are reached. It is understandable that the heart of the Jewish convert longs to reach his own people, just as Paul's did to the point where he was even willing to give up his own salvation. Even so, Paul could not reach the Jews because that was not his commission. The Gentile Church needs to take up the burden of reaching the Jews, and the Church desperately needs the converted Jews to help us reach them.

THE DISTORTION OF REALITY

The news media is one of the primary tools being used by the enemy to sow deception and division between peoples. Although this may not be their intent, it is the end result. The news itself is a gross distortion of reality. Only the most extreme events make the news and most of them are acts of violence. Good news does not sell, and even the good that makes the news is not a true perception of reality.

News of domestic violence is never balanced by news of the many happy families. The overwhelming majority of Americans today will do their jobs and go about their business in a normal manner, but none of that which is "normal" America will make the evening news. The news itself presents a very distorted caricature of life in America, or anywhere else.

Even the Christian media, trying to do an honest job of reporting the interesting events in the Church, often creates an unreal perception of Christianity for their own Christian readers. The average church in America is not like the churches that are newsworthy. The day-to-day ministries of the average church in the community is probably doing far more to accomplish a true advance for the gospel, but it is rarely spectacular enough to make the news. Even so, these average churches are also a much more accurate reflection of the true state of Christianity today, for good or for bad.

Unfortunately, even when there is no intention to distort the facts, the very nature of the modern media does distort reality. Even family-oriented sitcoms project families where almost every action or statement is either cute, funny, or dramatic. The truly normal family would make a very boring sitcom. When the average family compares their lives to those of the television family, they often become disappointed with what they have and who they are. The overall effect of this blurs reality and reduces our perceptions to "sound bites," in which we are being subtly trained only to respond to extremes.

Strongholds are basically lies that people believe. The more people that believe a falsehood, the more powerful that stronghold. The enemy is using the media to sow a demented perception of almost everything. The result will be that more and more of the extremes projected by the media will become normal behavior. Only the Church, which has been given the Spirit of Truth, has the grace and power required to tear down these strongholds of misconception and false judgments. The divinely powerful weapons with which we have been trusted were given to us for the purpose of tearing down strongholds and we must use them.

THE DECEPTION OF EXTREMES

Satan has been very successful in causing and maintaining division between people by encouraging us to judge other people groups by their most extreme elements. For example, the way that liberals look at conservatives and see the KKK or the way conservatives look at liberals and see communists. It is a primary strategy of the enemy to have us perceive one another through caricatures that the enemy has sown in our minds. This drives us farther apart and decreases the possibility of unity, which the enemy fears so much.

Few Christians today are of the nature that was demonstrated by the crusaders, but the world does tend to view us all according to the most extreme elements of the faith. We must also recognize that very few members of other religions, or ethnic groups, can be likened to the most extreme elements that we probably have viewed in the media.

Because the enemy's basic strategy is to sow division and misunderstanding by having us judge each other after projected images and caricatures, we must overcome this thought process by learning to judge other people after the Spirit and not after the flesh. We must not continue to receive our discernment, and in many cases even our information, from the media, but from the Holy Spirit.

WE KNOW IN PART

Men need women, and women need men. Blacks need whites, and whites need blacks. Denominations need each other. We all need each other. It was for this purpose that 1 Corinthians 13:9 states, "For we know in part, and we prophesy in part." Therefore, to have the complete picture, we must learn to put our little part together with the parts of others. We simply cannot make it through what is coming without unity, so we must learn what the rest of that chapter is about—love.

Love opens us up to seeing much more than we could otherwise see. Love is the foundation of all true vision, and true prophecy. Anything but love will distort our vision. One of the tragic mistakes genuine prophetic people make is thinking that their little part is the whole vision. But fortunately, love opens our hearts to understand others, and therefore receive from their perspective.

CHAPTER FIVE

THE TWO MINISTRIES

THE SCRIPTURES REVEAL that two acts occur continually before the throne of God—*intercession* and *accusation*. The conflict between these two is a focal point of the battle between the Kingdom of God and the kingdom of darkness. Because God has chosen to make the Church His dwelling place, and therefore, the place of His throne, it is in the heart of the Church that this battle now rages.

Jesus "always lives to make intercession" (Heb. 7:25). It is the fundamental nature of Jesus to be an intercessor, a priest. To the degree that we abide in Him, Jesus will use us to intercede. For this reason, His Church is called to be a "...house of prayer for all the nations" (Mk. 11:17).

Satan is called "the accuser of our brethren...who accuses them before our God day and night" (Rev. 12:10). To the degree that the enemy has access to our lives he will use us to accuse and criticize the brethren. Like the two trees in the

Garden, we must choose which of these we are going to partake of—intercession or accusation.

We may ask how satan could continue to accuse the saints before God if he has been thrown out of Heaven and no longer has access to the throne. The answer is that satan uses the saints, who do have access to the throne, to accomplish this diabolical work for him.

SATAN'S GREATEST VICTORY

Satan is called by many titles but certainly his most effective guise has been "accuser of the brethren." This title was given to him because of his effectiveness in getting brother to turn against brother. From the time that he entered the Garden to thwart the purpose of man, accusation has been his specialty. Even when there were just two brothers on earth, they could not get along. The presence of satan will always promote discord and division.

Satan's greatest victory over the Church is in turning the brethren against each other. *Accusation* has been his most effective and deadly tool in destroying the light, the power, and the witness of the Body of Christ. Our ability to accomplish our purpose in this world will be determined by the degree to which we can dispel our deadly enemy and learn to live for one another.

The greatest threat to satan's domain is the unity of the Church. The devil knows very well the awesome authority that Jesus has given to any two who will agree. He knows that with agreement between just two saints, the Father will give them what they ask. He understands that one saint can put a thousand to flight but two of them together can put ten thousand to flight. Unity does not just increase our spiritual authority, it exponentially multiplies it. Unfortunately, the enemy understands all of this much better than the Church does.

The access the accuser has to most believers is through their insecurity. This drives them to become territorial or possessive. The insecure are threatened by anything that they cannot control. The accuser may use many seemingly noble justifications for his attacks on others, such as to protect the truth or the sheep, but rarely has there been a division in the Church that was not rooted in territorial- or self-preservation.

The greater the authority or influence that one has in the Church, the bigger the target they make. Satan knows well that if he can sow territorial- or self-preservation in the heart of a spiritual leader, the leader will sow it in all of those under him, and the more destructive the division or sectarian spirit can become.

Ironically, the division that is caused by trying to protect our domains is the very thing that cuts us off from true spiritual authority and anointing. This ultimately results in our losing the very thing we are so desperately trying to preserve, which is an incontrovertible law of the spirit: "For whoever wishes to save his life shall lose it; but whoever loses his life for My sake shall find it" (Mt. 16:25). Isaiah addressed this issue in Isaiah 58:8-9:

> *Then your light will break out like the dawn, and your recovery will speedily spring forth; and your righteousness will go before you; the glory of the Lord will be your rear guard.*
>
> *Then you will call, and the Lord will answer; you will cry, and He will say, "Here I am." If you remove the yoke from your midst, the pointing of the finger, and speaking wickedness.*

We are promised that if we remove the yoke of criticism from our midst (which is portrayed as "the pointing of the finger, and speaking wickedness"), our light will break out, our healing will come speedily, the glory of the Lord will follow us, and He will answer our prayers. There is possibly nothing that can so radically change the Church, and the lives of individual believers, than having our criticisms changed into intercession. Likewise, it is probable that the addiction to criticism is the main reason why there is so little light, so little healing, so little of the glory of the Lord, and so little answered prayer in the Church today.

CRITICISM IS PRIDE

Criticism is one of the ultimate manifestations of pride because, whenever we criticize someone else, we assume we are superior to them. Pride brings that which any rational human being should fear the most—*God's resistance.* "...God resists the proud, but gives grace to the humble" (Jas. 4:6 NKJV). We would be better off having all the demons in hell resisting us than God!

Pride caused the first fall, and it has been a root in probably every fall from grace since. Peter's betrayal of the Lord is one of the great examples of how pride causes us to fall from grace. On the very same night that Peter betrayed the Lord, he earlier charged a Roman cohort to defend his Lord. Even though this was misguided zeal, it was impressive courage—a Roman cohort was composed of 800 men! Earlier when the Lord warned Peter of his impending denial of Him, Peter challenged the Son of God Himself, declaring, "They may all fall away from You but not me." Peter considered himself to be a man of courage and was willing to die for the Lord. He just did not know where the courage came from. The Lord did not cause Peter to fall that night; He just removed the grace by which he was standing. Then the fearless man who had charged a Roman cohort could not even stand before a servant girl!

None of us can stand at any moment except by the grace of God. This is more than a cliché—it is a basic biblical truth. When we condemn others who are having problems, we are putting ourselves in jeopardy of falling to the same sins. That is why Paul warned us: "Brethren, even if a man is caught *in any trespass,* you who are spiritual, restore such a one in a spirit of gentleness; each one looking to yourself, *lest you too be tempted*" (Gal. 6:1).

WHO ARE WE CRITICIZING?

When we criticize another Christian, we are actually saying that God's workmanship does not meet up to our standards— that we could do it better. When we criticize someone else's children, who takes offense? The parents! This is no less true of God. When we judge one of His people, we are judging Him. When we judge one of His leaders, we are actually judging *His* leadership. We are saying that He does not know what He is doing with the leadership that He is providing.

Such grumbling and complaining is the same problem that kept the first generation of the children of Israel from possessing their promised land. Their grumbling caused them to spend their entire lives wandering in dry places, and this is still the chief reason why so many Christians do not walk in the promises of God. We have been warned:

> *Do not speak against one another, brethren. He who speaks against a brother or judges his brother, speaks against the*

law and judges the law; but if you judge the law, you are not a doer of the law, but a judge of it.

There is only one Lawgiver and Judge, the One who is able to save and to destroy [when we judge the law, we judge the Lawgiver]*; but who are you who judge your neighbor?*

James 4:11-12

When we point the finger to criticize, we yoke ourselves:

Judge not, that you be not be judged.

For with what judgment you judge, you will be judged; and with the same measure you use, it will be measured back to you.

Matthew 7:1-2 NKJV

The text in Isaiah 58 implies that the primary reason for the darkness, lack of healing, unanswered prayer, and lack of the glory of God, is our own critical spirit, which is called "the pointing of the finger and speaking wickedness." Of the many people I have met with exceptional mantles of spiritual authority, but who were lacking in spiritual fruit, this characteristic always seemed to prevail in their lives. They had judged and criticized the ministries of others who were gaining influence, and had thereby disqualified themselves from the grace of God in that area. Our criticisms will bring us to poverty. "Death and life are in the power of the tongue, and those who love it will eat its fruit" (Prov. 18:21).

As Solomon observed:

But the path of the just is like the shining sun, that shines ever brighter unto the perfect day.

The way of the wicked is like darkness; they do not know what makes them stumble.

Proverbs 4:18-19 NKJV

If we are walking in righteousness, we walk in increasing light. On the other hand, those who stumble around in the dark seldom know the reason for that darkness, otherwise they would not be living in it. The critical person is usually critical of everyone but himself, and therefore, cannot see his own problems. The Lord stated that he is so busy looking for specks in the eyes of his brothers, he cannot see the big log in his own eye, which is the reason for his blindness.

STUMBLING BLOCKS

The Lord indicated that the very last thing we should ever want to be is a stumbling block. He said that it would be better for us not to have been born than to cause even one of His little ones to stumble. In the same conversation in which He warned us not to become a stumbling block (see Mt. 18), He gave clear instructions about how we are to deal with a brother or sister who is in sin—so that we will not become a stumbling block.

First, we must go to the person in private. If he rejects our counsel and only after he has rejected our counsel, do we go to him again with another brother. Only after he rejects the second counsel should we ever go before the rest of the church with the issue. If we do not follow this pattern, we will be in jeopardy of suffering a fate worse than the person who is in sin—becoming a stumbling block (see Mt. 18:1517).

This tendency toward unrighteous judgment in the Church is very possibly why many will come to the Lord on judgment day, having done many great things in His name, but will still hear those terrible words: "Depart from Me, you who practice lawlessness." By the Lord's own teachings, it would be very hard for us to overstate the importance of this terrible sin of unrighteous judgment (see Mt. 7:23).

I have heard numerous excuses for not following the Matthew 18 pattern for dealing with sin, such as: "I knew they would not listen to me," or "If they have a public ministry, we have a right to expose them publicly." However, the Lord did not say that we only had to comply with His instructions when we knew people would listen to us. He obviously implied that at least some would not hear, which is why there are the subsequent steps.

As far as the public ministry excuse goes, this is also flawed logic, because every ministry is public, at least to some degree. Who determines the degree to which it has become so public that it frees us from compliance with God's Word? The Lord gave no such conditions. Those who take such liberties with the clear commandments given by Jesus Himself are by this logic claiming to have authority to add to the Word of God.

If we believe a man with a large ministry is in sin, and we are not able to persuade him with our discernment, then we must not be the one to execute the judgment. Do not accuse, but intercede! The Lord is able to judge His own house and He is able to make a way for us if we are the ones He wants to use. If He does not make a way for us, we must trust Him to do it in His own time. Again, this is to protect us from coming under a judgment that is more severe than the brother who is in sin.

If we have not followed the Lord's prescribed manner for dealing with a brother who is in sin, we have absolutely no right to talk about it to anyone else, much less to go public with it. It should not even be shared to get another's opinion on the matter. What we may call getting someone else's opinion, God usually calls gossip. He is not fooled, and we will pay the price for such indiscretions. Even if we follow every one of the steps in Matthew 18, and determine that we should bring an issue before the church, our goal must always be to save the brother from his sin, not to expose him.

CHAPTER SIX

LOVE AND VISION

IN LIGHT OF THE LAST CHAPTER'S DISCUSSION, let us not become petty with our challenges to the presumed sin in a brother's life, because "...love covers a multitude of sins" (1 Pet. 4:8). The majority of us still have a few hundred things wrong with us. The Lord is usually dealing with one or two of them at a time because that is all we can take. It is one of satan's strategies to distract us into trying to deal with the other 300 problems simultaneously, resulting in frustration and defeat. Matthew 18 was not given as a club for our use to beat up on each other, or even as permission to let a brother know how he offended us. If we have love, we will cover most of those sins, unless they are bringing unnecessary injury to our brother. We must use this Scripture, and indeed all Scripture, in love, not out of self-preservation or retaliation.

Of course, the Lord Jesus Himself is our perfect model. When He corrected the seven churches in Revelation, He gave us an example for bringing correction to the Church. He first praised each church and highlighted what they were doing right. He then straightforwardly addressed their problems. Incredibly,

He even gave Jezebel time to repent! He then gave each church a wonderful promise of reward for overcoming their problems. The Lord never changes. When He brings correction today, it always comes wrapped in encouragement, hope, and promises.

The "accuser of the brethren" is also trying to bring correction to the Church. However, his methods and goals are obviously quite different. Jesus encourages and gives hope; satan condemns and imparts hopelessness. Jesus builds us up, so we can handle the correction; satan tears us down, trying to get us to quit. Jesus loves us and wants to lift us up; satan's goal is always destruction.

Discernment

We must walk in discernment, as Paul declared, "...Do you not judge those who are within the church?" (1 Cor. 5:12). However, we must be careful to note that criticism can be rooted in true discernment. Those we criticize may well be in error. The pastors mentioned previously who criticized the way others raised money through manipulation, hype, and sometimes outright deception, were accurate in their discernment. The issue is how we deal with what we discern—are we going to use it to accuse or to intercede? Which ministry are we a part of? How we deal with discernment can determine the outcome of our own spiritual lives.

A worthless person, a wicked man, walks with a perverse mouth;

He winks with his eyes, he shuffles his feet, he points with his fingers;

Perversity is in his heart. He devises evil continually, he sows discord.

Therefore his calamity shall come suddenly; suddenly he shall be broken without remedy.

Proverbs 6:12-15 NKJV

Much of what has been paraded as discernment is nothing less than suspicion—a pseudo-spiritual disguise used to mask territorial preservation. Regardless of whether we have the spiritual gift of discernment or not, we have clear guidelines in the Book of James for discerning the source of wisdom. Had we heeded them, it could have preserved the Church from some of our most humiliating failures:

Who is wise and understanding among you? Let him show by good conduct that his works are done in the meekness of wisdom.

But if you have bitter envy and self-seeking in your hearts, do not boast and lie against the truth.

This wisdom does not descend from above, but is earthly, sensual, demonic.

For where envy and self-seeking exist, confusion and every evil thing will be there.

But the wisdom that is from above is first pure, then peaceable, gentle, willing to yield, full of mercy and good fruits, without partiality and without hypocrisy.

Now the fruit of righteousness is sown in peace by those who make peace.

James 3:13-18 NKJV

We are saved by grace, and we will always need all the grace we can get to make it through this life. If we want to receive more grace, we had better learn to give grace, for we reap what we sow. If we expect to receive mercy, we must start sowing mercy. Most of us will need all the mercy we can get. The very last thing we want to do is come before the Lord with our brother's blood on our hands, just as He warned:

> *You have heard that it was said to those of old, "You shall not murder," and whoever murders will be in danger of the judgment.*
>
> *But I say to you that whoever is angry with his brother without a cause shall be in danger of the judgment. And whoever says to his brother, "Raca!"* [empty head] *shall be in danger of the council. But whoever says, "You fool!" shall be in danger of hell fire.*
>
> *Therefore if you bring your gift to the altar, and there remember that your brother has something against you,*
>
> *leave your gift there before the altar, and go your way. First be reconciled to your brother, and then come and offer your gift.*
>
> *Agree with your adversary quickly, while you are on the way with him, lest your adversary deliver you to the judge, the judge hand you over to the officer, and you be thrown into prison* [bondage].
>
> *Assuredly, I say to you, you will by no means get out of there till you have paid the last penny.*
>
> Matthew 5:21-26 NKJV

It is clear by this warning that, if we have been guilty of slandering a brother, we should forget about our offerings to the Lord until we have been reconciled to our brother. He links slandering and offerings together because we think that our sacrifices and offerings can compensate for such sins, but they never will. We will stay locked in the prisons we have built for ourselves with our judgments, until we have paid the last cent, or until we are reconciled to the brother that we slandered.

The Lord said that when He returned, He would judge between the sheep and the goats (see Mt. 25:31-46). Those who are judged sheep will inherit the Kingdom and eternal life. Those who are designated goats will be sent to eternal judgment. The separation will be determined by how each group has treated the Lord, which will be determined by how they have treated His people. John stated it:

If someone says, "I love God," and hates his brother, he is a liar; for the one who does not love his brother whom he has seen, cannot love God whom he has not seen.

1 John 4:20

Everyone who hates his brother is a murderer; and you know that no murderer has eternal life abiding in him.

We know love by this, that He laid down His life for us; and we ought to lay down our lives for the brethren.

1 John 3:15-16

If we really have Christ's Spirit we will also possess His nature. How many of us, knowing that our best friends, whom we had poured our lives into for three and a half years, were about to desert us and even deny that they knew us, would have "earnestly desired" to have one last meal with them? Our Lord's love for His disciples has never been conditional upon their doing right. Even though He knew they were about to desert Him and deny Him, He loved them to the end—He even gave His life for them. When He saw our sin, He did not criticize us; He laid down His life for us. He has commanded us to love with that same love.

Winning the War Between Generations

One of the great tragedies of Church history has been the way leaders of each move of God have become opposers and persecutors of succeeding moves. To date this trend has not failed. The Lord uses this to help purify and work humility into those He is about to release with increasing power and authority, but this is still a great tragedy. Numerous leaders have spent their lives serving faithfully only to finish as vessels for the accuser, who makes them a stumbling block for the next move.

What is it that causes leaders of one move to become opposers of the next move? There are several factors involved, which we must understand and be delivered of, or we will find ourselves guilty of the same actions. We might think and say we would never do such things, but that is what previous church leaders had thought and said as well. "Therefore let him who thinks he stands take heed that he does not fall" (1 Cor. 10:12). The pride that causes us to assume we will not do such a thing is one of the factors that leads to doing it.

This problem actually precedes Church history and goes all the way back to the very first two brothers born into this world. John observed why the older could not bear the younger:

> For this is the message which you have heard from the beginning, that we should love one another;
>
> **Not as Cain, who was of the evil one, and slew his brother. And for what reason did he slay him? Because his deeds were evil, and his brother's were righteous.**
>
> 1 John 3:11-12

Each new move of the Holy Spirit has resulted in the restoration of more light to the Church. This light is not new truth, but truth that was lost to the Church through the Dark Ages of her history. Regardless of what we call our opposition, the basic reason for most of it is jealousy. Those in leadership, or those who have been faithful to the light that they have had for a time, have difficulty believing that anyone is more worthy, or that the Lord would want to use anyone but them for further restoration of His truth and purposes.

There is only one remedy that will keep leaders from ultimately falling to this terrible trap—to seek the humility and nature of John the Baptist. This man was one of the greatest types of true spiritual ministry. His whole purpose in life was to prepare the way for Jesus, to point to Him, then to decrease as the greater One increased. It was John's joy to see the One who followed him going further than he went.

On the other hand, if we are part of an emerging generation, we must realize that the pride of thinking we are better than those who went before us can disqualify us from going any further ourselves. The only commandment with a promise is that which commands us to honor our fathers and mothers, referring to both our natural and spiritual fathers and mothers. The promise is to "remain long in the land which the Lord has given you." Our spiritual longevity is directly related to this one issue.

When I inquired of the Lord many years ago how to honor my spiritual fathers and mothers, the Lord replied that just as Israel considered it an honor to drink from the wells that their ancestors had dug, I could also honor my spiritual fathers and mothers by drinking from their spiritual wells. I began to do this, and have found treasures of wisdom and knowledge that are beyond earthly value.

This is also one of the many ways that the Lord has saved the best wine for last. For example, I have spent nearly 30 years accumulating the knowledge and understanding condensed into this book, which you can read in a few hours! Many of the books and messages given to us by our spiritual fathers and mothers contain an entire lifetime of experience and wisdom that we can receive in a couple of hours or days. How will we ever be able to thank them enough, or thank the Lord enough for letting us live in these times?

Scientists today would be very limited in developing technology if they had to begin by reinventing the wheel and taking every step over themselves from that point on. We would still be living in the Stone Age. The increase of knowledge that has created such technological advancement is mirrored by a similar spiritual increase of knowledge that is preparing to release a generation into realms of the Spirit that the Lord promised would enable us to do things that He did and even greater things. We must not miss this unprecedented opportunity. But none of it would be possible without what Jesus did, and what those who have gone before us did. To fail to honor them is to sever ourselves from the faith and humility that enables us to receive it.

Chapter Seven

The Heart
of the Freedom Fighter

In order for the Church to advance, future spiritual leaders must become "spiritual eunuchs." A eunuch's whole purpose was to prepare the bride for the king. It was not possible for the eunuch to desire the bride, but his joy was wrapped up in his king's joy. When we use the ministry in order to build a reputation for ourselves or to find those who will serve us, we will not be of the same authority of Christ. Paul exhorted us:

> *Do nothing from selfishness or empty conceit, but with humility of mind let each of you regard one another as more important than himself;*

> *do not merely look out for your own personal interests, but also for the interests of others.*

> *Have this attitude in yourselves which was also in Christ Jesus,*

> *who, although He existed in the form of God, did not regard equality with God a thing to be grasped,*

but emptied Himself, taking the form of a bond-servant, and being made in the likeness of men.

Being found in appearance as a man, He humbled Himself by becoming obedient to the point of death, even death on a cross.

Therefore also God highly exalted Him, and bestowed on Him the name which is above every name.

Philippians 2:3-9

This Scripture is the pattern that Jesus set for everyone who would follow Him in leadership. Humility comes before authority and position. He said in Luke 14:11: "For everyone who exalts himself will be humbled, and he who humbles himself shall be exalted." A key word here is "everyone." James added, "Humble yourselves in the presence of the Lord, and He will exalt you" (Jas. 4:10). Peter stated, "Humble yourselves, therefore, under the mighty hand of God, that He may exalt you at the proper time" (1 Pet. 5:6). In all of these texts, we see that it is our job to humble ourselves and it is the Lord's job to do the exalting. It is clear that if we try to do His job, He will do our job, and He can do either one of them much better than we can.

The evil spirits of self-promotion and territorial preservation have done much damage to the Church. They have caused many potentially great leaders to be disqualified from receiving further anointing and authority. The influence we gain by our own self-promotion or manipulation will become a stumbling block that keeps us from attaining positions that God would otherwise give to us.

It has not always been the older generation of leaders that were the stumbling block for the new. The new generation can be just as guilty of causing the previous one to stumble! The very arrogance of presuming that we are the new generation reveals a pride that God has to resist. This presumption is a humiliating slap in the face to men and women who have given their lives to faithfully serving the Lord and His people.

Jesus did not ridicule John the Baptist for being a part of the old order—He honored him. Jesus even submitted Himself to John's ministry. This submission did not mean that He allowed John to control Him; instead He acknowledged John and esteemed him and his work.

Later, when Jesus was asked the source of His authority, he pointed to John and asked His inquisitors if they knew from where John's baptism came. The answer to His question was the answer to their question. John was the last of an order—he was there to represent all of those who had prophesied the coming Messiah from the very beginning. John was their representative, acknowledging Jesus as the One of whom they all had spoken, and that He was indeed the Lamb of God. Jesus acknowledged the baptism of those who had gone before Him as the credentials of His authority.

Those who will be of the new generation must likewise submit to the ministry of those who have gone before them if they are to fulfill all righteousness. We are presently in the midst of seeing a new spiritual generation emerge. It is also apparent that the previous movements are beginning to decrease as the new order emerges. However, it is crucial that the leaders of the new order honor those who went before them, or they will be in jeopardy of disqualifying themselves from advancing in the Kingdom. The arrogance of the new order can be just as much an affront to the Spirit of God as that of the old who resist God in the new things He begins to do.

Why the Abused Become the Abusers

As previously mentioned when discussing the "tyranny of the familiar," one of the baffling questions is why people get trapped in cycles of oppression and bondage and refuse to go free even when they are able to. Abused children who swear that they will never grow up like their parents inevitably grow up to be abusers. Why is it that accused saints grow up to become accusers? The answer is the same for both. Abused children usually grow up determined not to be like their parents, thus they become reactionary, which does not lead to grace, but can actually nurture bitterness. This ultimately results in their becoming just like their parents. Only humility and forgiveness can ever break that cycle.

The sins of the parents will become the sins of the children until we receive the grace of the cross. Because God gives grace to the humble, we must understand that we will take on the sins of our parents without His help. That is one reason why many of the great leaders in Scripture prayed to be forgiven for the sins of their fathers.

Elijah Must Come

There will be a spiritual generation that will be persecuted just as every one before it; however, they will not go on to persecute the next generation. This movement will not be subject to the "pride of generations," assuming that all things will be concluded with them. Those of this generation will find the grace of the cross and will forgive from the heart, those who mistreat them. They will perceive and even hope that their children, spiritual and natural, may go farther in Christ than they did, and they will rejoice in it. They will give their lives to making the way of the next generation as smooth as possible, and then they will rejoice to decrease as that generation arises. This will be the generation of the spirit of Elijah who will return the hearts of the fathers to the sons, and the hearts of the sons to the fathers.

Our ability to be the generation that prepares the way for the Lord and His ultimate purposes will be determined by which of the two ministries we become a part of—accusation or intercession. Let us now remove the terrible yoke of "pointing the finger" from our midst and begin turning our criticisms into intercession.

> *Then your light will break out like the dawn, and your recovery will speedily spring forth; and your righteousness will go before you; the glory of the Lord will be your rear guard.*
>
> *Then you will call, and the Lord will answer; you will cry, and He will say, "Here I am." If you remove the yoke from your midst, the pointing of the finger, and speaking wickedness...*
>
> *And the Lord will continually guide you, and satisfy your desire in scorched places, and give strength to your bones; and you will be like a watered garden, and like a spring of water whose waters do not fail.*
>
> *Those from among you will rebuild the ancient ruins; you will raise up the age-old foundations; and you will be called the repairer of the breach, the restorer of the streets in which to dwell.*
>
> Isaiah 58:8-9, 11-12

According to this text, the "pointing of the finger," or that critical spirit, is the reason why there is so little light, healing, answered prayer, or the glory of the Lord revealed. Turning our criticisms into intercession can be the one thing that most radically changes the life, power, and glory that we experience in the Lord. It can do it for the Church, and for us as individuals. If we do this, we will be those who restore the age-old foundations, and repair the breach between God and man, and therefore between men and other men. Then the glory will come. All we are doing is trading our bitterness for glory. Isn't it time to do this?

Because love covers a multitude of sins, let us determine that we are going to grow in love by covering other people's sins against us. Start with the person who irritates you the most, whether it is your spouse, boss, pastor, etc. Now consider what it is they do that irritates you the most. This is your greatest opportunity to grow in love. Determine that you are going to cover that which irritates you and start praying for the Lord to bless that person. Then start using other things that irritate you as a call to grow in love. If you do this, your life will radically change, and so will the lives of all who are close to you.

PART TWO

THE STRONGHOLD
OF WITCHCRAFT

CHAPTER EIGHT

UNDERSTANDING WITCHCRAFT

THE PRACTICE OF WITCHCRAFT has dramatically increased throughout the world in recent years. One of the expressed goals of many involved in this movement is to destroy Christianity. Many Christians are presently suffering some form of attack from those who practice witchcraft. Discerning the nature of these attacks, and knowing how to overcome them, is becoming crucial for all believers. The only way that a Christian can be defeated is through our own ignorance or complacency. As we maintain our position in Christ, taking on the full armor of God and remaining vigilant, we will not only stand, but will prevail against any attack from hell.

WHAT IS WITCHCRAFT?

Witchcraft is counterfeit spiritual authority; it is using a spirit other than the Holy Spirit to dominate, manipulate, or control others.

In Galatians 5:20, the apostle Paul named witchcraft, or "sorcery," as one of the deeds of the flesh. Though witchcraft has *its origin in the carnal nature of man,* it usually degenerates quickly into demonic power. Using emotional pressure to manipulate others is a basic form of witchcraft. Using hype or soul power to enlist service, even for the work of God, is witchcraft. When businessmen scheme to find pressure points while pursuing a deal, it can also be considered witchcraft. Many of the manipulative tactics promoted as sales techniques in marketing are basic forms of witchcraft.

The primary defense against counterfeit spiritual authority is to walk in true spiritual authority. Establishing our lives on truth and trusting in the Lord to accomplish what concerns us are essential keys to becoming free from the influence and pressure of witchcraft.

It is written that Jesus is seated upon the throne of David. This indicates that David established a position of true spiritual authority that would ultimately be manifested in the Kingdom of God. David did for spiritual authority what Abraham did for faith.

How did David establish a seat of true authority? Basically, he refused to take authority or seek influence for himself, but completely trusted in God to establish him in the position that He had ordained for him. David did not lift his own hand to seek recognition or influence, and neither should we if we want to walk in true spiritual authority rather than mere human political power.

Any authority or influence that we gain by our own manipulation or self-promotion will become a stumbling block to us and will hinder our ability to receive true authority from God. If we want to walk in true spiritual authority like David, we will have to utterly trust in the Lord to establish us in it in His time. As Peter exhorted, "Humble yourselves, therefore, under the mighty hand of God, *that He may exalt you at the proper time*" (1 Pet. 5:6).

Einstein once made the observation that "Premature responsibility breeds superficiality." This may be even more useful to us than his Theory of Relativity. There is possibly nothing more devastating to our calling and potential for walking in true ministry than seeking influence or authority prematurely.

When the Lord promotes, He also supplies the grace and wisdom to carry the authority. There is no greater security available than knowing that God is the one who has established our ministry. Few things can breed insecurity faster than trying to maintain a position that we have gained by our own promotion or manipulation. This is the root of most of the territorial preservation and division that exist in the Body of Christ.

Being established in true spiritual authority is a fortress that simply cannot be penetrated by the enemy. "...The God of peace will soon crush Satan under your feet..." (Rom. 16:20). When we know that we have been given our authority and have been established in our position by God, we have a peace that will utterly crush the enemy's attacks against us.

In contrast, when we establish ourselves in a position of authority, we will have little peace. The more our illegally gained influence increases, the more striving and manipulating it will take to hold it together. Anything that we do through manipulation, hype, or soul power, regardless of seemingly noble goals, is doomed to ultimate failure.

Therefore, the first principle in being delivered from the influence of witchcraft is to repent of all the ways that we ourselves have used it in our own lives and ministries. Satan cannot cast out satan. Witchcraft, in even its most evil and diabolical forms such as black magic, will have an open door into our lives if we ourselves are using manipulation to control others or gain position.

Although we may try to justify using such devices in order to build the Church, God is not fooled and neither is the enemy. What God is building is not raised up by might nor by power, but by His Spirit. Whatever we build by any other means is an affront to the cross, and will ultimately oppose that which the Spirit is doing. The flesh wars against the Spirit, regardless of how good we try to make the flesh look.

Spiritual Maturity

One of the primary ways that the Lord works in our lives to help us overcome our tendency to use manipulative tactics is by allowing us to endure rejection. Rejection is the one thing we hate the most, and it even seems that the Lord's greatest trial on the cross was the rejection He suffered when the Father turned away from Him. Because rejection can be such a difficult trial, it can also be a great opportunity to be delivered from the fear of man, and the fear of rejection, which can devastate any life or ministry.

Almost everyone in ministry must endure considerable rejection and misunderstanding. Learning to overcome rejection, by forgiving and praying for our persecutors just as the Lord did, is essential if we are to walk in the Spirit and exercise true spiritual authority. If we are to accomplish the purposes of God, we must come to the level of maturity where, "the love of Christ controls us" (2 Cor. 5:14). Love does not take into account the wrongs we have suffered and is not motivated by rejection, which drives us to retaliate or try to prove ourselves. Such reactions are the first step in a fall from true authority. As the Lord Jesus stated,

He who speaks from himself seeks his own glory [literally "recognition"]; *but He who is seeking the glory* [recognition] *of the One who sent Him, He is true, and there is no unrighteousness in Him.*

John 7:18

There are few things that will more quickly destroy our ability to walk in true spiritual authority than self-seeking, self-promotion, or self-preservation. On the other hand, learning to deal with rejection is mandatory if we are to walk in a true ministry. Rejection provides an opportunity for us to grow in grace and die a little more to ambition, pride, and other motives that so quickly color our revelation. If we embrace rejection as a discipline of the Lord, we will grow in grace and love. If we rebel against this discipline, we may enter into witchcraft.

The Fear of Man Leads to Witchcraft

King Saul is a good example of how a man with a true commission from God can fall into this counterfeit spiritual authority. When he was commanded to wait for Samuel before offering the sacrifice, he succumbed to pressure and offered it prematurely, saying, "...I saw that the people were scattering from me...and that the Philistines were assembling..." (1 Sam. 13:11). This is the same point where most fall from true authority—when they begin to fear the people or the circumstances more than they fear God. When we start to fear the people leaving more than we fear God leaving, we will have departed from true faith.

Because witchcraft is basically rooted in the fear of man, and "the fear of man brings a snare..." (Prov. 29:25), those who begin to operate in witchcraft are trapped because fear has snared them. The bigger the project or ministry that we have built with hype, manipulation, or control spirits, the more we will fear anyone or anything that we cannot manipulate or control. Those who are caught in this deadly trap will fear those who walk in the true anointing and authority, because those who walk in true spiritual authority are the least affected by manipulation or the spirit of control.

Saul became enraged at David and was consumed with destroying him, even though David was at the time but "a single flea" (1 Sam. 24:14). As the manipulation and control spirits increase their dominion, so will the paranoia of those who are trapped within their grasp. Such people will become irrationally consumed by an attempt to drive out or destroy anyone who threatens their control.

Those who receive their authority, recognition, or security from men, like Saul, will end up in the witch's house. Samuel warned Saul that "rebellion is as the sin of witchcraft" (1 Sam. 15:23 NKJV). When one in spiritual authority rebels against the Holy Spirit, the void will be filled by the counterfeit spiritual authority of witchcraft. This may begin as a simple reliance upon hype and soul power, but without repentance it can end up in the most diabolical forms of presumption and rebellion, as we see in the case of King Saul. Persecuting those who were faithful to the Lord, Saul killed the true priests and spent one of his last nights in the house of a witch as the natural conclusion to the direction his life had taken.

Spiritual authority is a dangerous occupation. If we are wise, like David, we will not seek a position of authority, and we will not even take one which is offered until we are certain that the Lord is the one giving it. Satan tempts everyone called by God with the same temptation he offered to Jesus—if we will bow down to him and his ways, he will give us authority over kingdoms. God has called us to rule over kingdoms too, but His way leads to the cross. The authority He offers us can only be attained if we become servants of all. Satan's temptation is to offer the quick and easy path to the same place to which God has in fact called us.

PRESUMPTION KILLS

One of the most frequent phrases attributed to David's life was, "David inquired of the Lord..." (1 Sam. 30:8). On the few occasions when David made major decisions without inquiring of the Lord, the consequences were devastating. The higher the position of authority, the more dangerous it is, and the more people are affected by even seemingly insignificant decisions. True spiritual authority is not an honor to be sought; it is a burden to be carried. Many who seek authority and influence do not know what they are asking for. Immaturity can be our doom if authority is given to us before our time.

Even though David lived a thousand years before the age of grace, he knew the Lord's grace and lived by it. Yet he still made mistakes that cost thousands of lives. It was probably because Solomon had observed God's grace in his father's life that caused him to desire wisdom above all else to rule over God's people. Anyone called to a position of leadership in the Church must have the same devotion. Even if we are not in a position of spiritual authority, presumption can kill us. If we are in a position of authority, presumption will almost certainly lead to our fall and can lead to the fall of many others as well.

The gift of a word of knowledge can be an awesome demonstration of power, but those who are called to walk in spiritual authority would do well to seek words of wisdom even more than words of knowledge. We need demonstrations of power and words of knowledge to accomplish the work of the Lord, but it is essential that we also have the wisdom to use them properly.

HUMILITY IS A SAFETY NET

Those who attain prominence before humility will almost certainly fall. Therefore, if we have wisdom, we will seek humility before position. True authority operates on the grace of God, and the more authority we walk in, the more grace we will need. *We only have true spiritual authority to the degree that the King lives within us.* True spiritual authority is not position; it is grace. Counterfeit spiritual authority stands on its position instead of grace. Jesus is the highest spiritual authority, and He used His position to lay down His life. He commanded those who would come after Him to take up their crosses and do the same.

PROTECTION FROM CHARISMATIC WITCHCRAFT

Those in leadership must not only be wary of using witchcraft, they must also be aware that they will be the primary target of those who do. Witchcraft thus is an enemy we must guard against from within and without. It is just as subtle when it attacks from without as when it takes ground from within. This form of sorcery is seldom what we call black magic, but is usually a form of "white witchcraft." Those who practice it are often well-meaning people who do not have the confidence to be straightforward, and have therefore, fallen to subtle forms of manipulation to gain influence.

One prominent form of white witchcraft, which is common in the Church, can be described as "charismatic witchcraft." This has nothing to do with the Charismatic Movement, but is a pseudo-spirituality. It often uses this guise to gain influence or control of others or situations. It is a source of many false prophecies, dreams, and visions that can ultimately destroy or neutralize a church, or bring the leadership to the point where they overreact so as to despise prophecy altogether. Those using this form of witchcraft will almost always think that they have the mind of the Lord which gives them the greater authority. They will therefore conclude that the leadership, or anyone else who contradicts them, are the ones in rebellion.

JEZEBEL

Jezebel is an archetype of witchcraft in Scripture. She used her power to control her husband Ahab, the king, and therefore had the real authority over Israel. She was also able to bring such depression upon Elijah that he sought death over life even after his greatest spiritual victory. There is power in witchcraft. Those who are ignorant of it, or who presumptuously disregard its potential to affect them, are very often brought down by it. Many churches, ministries, movements, and even revivals have been stopped and/or destroyed by this evil. All who walk in true spiritual authority must understand it, or it will become a significant threat to all that they accomplish.

Jezebel may have easily overpowered Ahab, but Elijah was certainly no wimp. He single-handedly confronted and destroyed more than eight hundred false prophets in one of the greatest demonstrations of God's power over evil in all of history. Yet immediately after this, one woman operating in the power of witchcraft was able to send the great prophet fleeing in discouragement. This story reveals the kind of power to discourage that witchcraft can have on anyone.

How can this happen? Compared to the power of God, all the power of the evil one would not even register on the scale! The newest babe in Christ has more power dwelling in him than all the antichrists put together. How is it that we can still be overcome by evil? It is because satan does not confront God's people with power; *he distracts and seduces them with deception.*

Compared to the eight hundred false prophets, who was this one woman to challenge Elijah? Certainly he could have destroyed her power even more easily than he had destroyed the power of the false prophets. It was not rational for Elijah to have become so discouraged because of Jezebel's threat, but that is precisely the point: This attack did not come through reasoning; it was a spiritual attack. Reasoning usually has little to do with the power of witchcraft.

Jezebel slammed Elijah immediately after his greatest victory and it overpowered him. We will often be most vulnerable to this kind of an attack after a great victory because it is then that we tend to drop our guard and become most open to pride. Our first defense against the attacks of the enemy through witchcraft, or any other tactic, should be to maintain the humility of knowing that we are standing only by God's grace. Pride leaves a breach in our armor that the enemy can easily penetrate.

CHAPTER NINE

THE STINGS OF WITCHCRAFT

THE ATTACKS OF WITCHCRAFT USUALLY COME in a series of stings. The successive stings are meant to hit the very places where we have been weakened by the previous stings. In this way they build upon each other until the cumulative effect overwhelms the target. The stings of witchcraft usually come in the following order:

1. Discouragement
2. Confusion
3. Depression
4. Loss of Vision
5. Disorientation
6. Withdrawal
7. Despair
8. Defeat

This process can happen quickly, as it did with Elijah, but it usually works more slowly, which makes it even more difficult to discern. However, if we know the enemy's schemes, we will not continue to be subject to them. When these symptoms begin to make inroads into our lives, we must identify them and resist the enemy until he flees. If we do not resist him, we will be the ones fleeing just like Elijah.

The source of witchcraft used against us may not always be through the obvious satanic cults or New Age operatives. It can come from well-meaning, though deceived, Christians. These are the ones who start praying against leaders instead of for them. These misguided prayers have power because whatever is released on earth is released in Heaven, and whatever is bound on earth is bound in Heaven. If intercession is motivated by a spirit of control or manipulation, it is witchcraft and can have the same devastating power as black magic.

Other sources of charismatic witchcraft can be such things as gossip, political maneuvering, and jealousy; and they can have an effect on us whether we allow ourselves to be manipulated by them or not. For example, consider the result if we refuse to be manipulated by someone who has a control spirit, but allow ourselves to become resentful or bitter toward that person. In such a case, the enemy has still caused us to fall, and the discouragement, disorientation, and depression will come upon us just as surely as if we had submitted to the control spirit.

We are defeated by the enemy when he can get us to respond in any spirit other than the Holy Spirit, whose fruit is love, joy, peace, etc. (see Gal. 5:22-23). The enemy's strategy is to cause us to depart from the fruit of the Holy Spirit and try to combat him in our own strength. Remember that satan cannot cast out satan, and resentment will never cast out Jezebel—it will only increase her power.

Therefore, the basic strategy we must use to begin freeing ourselves from the power of witchcraft is to *bless those who curse us*. This does not mean that we bless their works, but that we pray for them and not against them. If the enemy can get us to retaliate, he will then have succeeded in causing us to use the same spirit, and we will have multiplied the very evil we were trying to cast out.

We are not warring against flesh and blood, and the weapons of our warfare are not carnal but spiritual. When we begin to pray blessings upon the people who are attacking us, then the evil power of control and manipulation is broken over both them and us. We must not return evil for evil, but we must *overcome evil with good.*

DISCERNING THE STINGS OF WITCHCRAFT

Sting 1—Discouragement

Everyone gets discouraged at times, and it can be for many different reasons. Discouragement is not always the result of witchcraft being used against us. However, if we become subject to increasing discouragement for no apparent reason, witchcraft should be considered as a possible source. When your difficulties seem insurmountable and you want to give up, even though matters are really not any worse than usual, you are probably coming under spiritual attack. The enemy's attempt to afflict you with discouragement is meant to weaken you for the next level of attack, which is:

Sting 2—Confusion

Again, we must look for a general and increasing "spirit of confusion" for which there is no apparent reason. Here we begin to lose our clarity about what we have been called to do, which of course will weaken our resolve. This confusion is meant to compound our discouragement, making us even weaker and more vulnerable to further attack, which will usually come in the form of:

Sting 3—Depression

This is a deeper problem than simple discouragement. It is an unshakable dread that comes as a result of the combined effect of discouragement and confusion, along with a general negligence in spiritual disciplines that has usually slipped in by this time. Depression will become an increasingly prevalent problem in the last days, and we must gain victory over it. If we do not, it will quickly lead to the next sting:

Sting 4—Loss of Vision

This is the goal of the previous stings and it works to increase their effect. Here we begin to doubt that God has called us to the task in the first place. The only way that we can sail through the storm of confusion is to hold our course, but we cannot hold our course if we do not know where we are going. We will not try to hold our course if we begin to think it was wrong for us to ever pursue our vision in the first place. Such a loss in vision will lead to our drifting in circles at the time when we most need to "make straight paths for your feet..." (Heb. 12:13). This sets us up for the next level of assault:

Sting 5—Disorientation

The combined result of depression, confusion, and loss of vision is usually disorientation. By this time, not only have we forgotten the course we are supposed to be holding, but we have even lost our ability to read the compass. The Scriptures will no longer speak to us, and it is a struggle to trust the Lord's voice or receive much encouragement from even the most anointed teaching or preaching. This is the point of spiritual incapacitation, the inability to function, which results in:

Sting 6—Withdrawal

When disorientation sets in, it is tempting to withdraw or retreat from our purpose in the ministry, our fellowship with the rest of the Church, and often from our families and others we are close to. Withdrawal will result in:

Sting 7—Despair

Withdrawal from the battle leads quickly to hopelessness and despair. Without hope we can easily be taken out by the enemy, either through temptation, sickness, or death. Science has proven that when hope is removed, even the most healthy person will quickly deteriorate and die. But with hope, men and women have lived long past the point when a normal body would have quit. Despair will always lead to:

Sting 8—Defeat

The enemy's purpose is to weaken us so that we begin to fall farther and farther behind; then we can be more easily picked off. In Scripture the Amalekites typified satan and his hordes. It was the practice of the Amalekites to attack the weak and defenseless. As the camp of Israel crossed the wilderness, the Amalekites picked off the loners or stragglers who fell behind the rest of the camp.

Through witchcraft the enemy seeks to weaken believers so that they will begin to fall behind the rest of the camp and become easy prey. Israel was warned that there would be perpetual war with the Amalekites. When Israel's kings were commanded to fight them, they were also commanded to utterly destroy them and not take any spoil. We have a perpetual war against satan, and we cannot take any prisoners. Neither can we use that which is his in the service of God.

King Saul disobeyed this command, keeping Agag, king of the Amalekites, alive and also keeping some of the spoil "to sacrifice to the Lord..." (1 Sam. 15:15). This was a failure of the most foolish kind for one called to lead God's people. In those days, keeping a rival king alive after a battle was only done for one of two reasons: to make him an ally or to make him a slave. Saul foolishly thought that he could make the one who personified satan himself into an ally or a slave.

It was no accident that it was an Amalekite who killed Saul and carried the news of Saul's death to David. This Amalekite thought that the news would be pleasing to David, but David was discerning and had him killed (see 2 Sam. 1:1-16). If we do not obey the Lord and utterly destroy the enemy we battle, he will eventually finish us off. There can be no alliance with the enemy; he and his hordes must be utterly destroyed. Neither let us be foolish enough to think that we can use the enemy as our slave; in his guile he will quickly turn the tables.

Witchcraft is being used against the Church. Many who have failed to recognize it have been defeated, losing their vision, their ministry, their families, and even their lives. This is not sensationalism; it is fact. Paul said that we do not wrestle against flesh and blood, but against principalities and powers (see Eph. 6:12). Wrestling is the closest form of combat. The enemy is going to fight, and he is going to wrestle with us. If we decide that we are just not going to fight, we will get pinned!

As Christians, we have no option as to whether or not we are going to do spiritual warfare—if we want to survive, we must fight. But how do we combat this witchcraft? We must first look at the basic principle of spiritual warfare required for every victory.

CHAPTER TEN

VICTORY OVER WITCHCRAFT

IN REVELATION 12:11 WE SEE that the saints overcome satan by:

1. the blood of the Lamb,
2. the word of their testimony, and
3. when they did not love their lives even unto death.

We overcome by the blood of the Lamb as we take our stand on what He has already accomplished for us by the cross. The victory has already been won and there is no way we can lose, if we abide in Him.

The word of our testimony is the Scriptures. Every time the enemy challenged Jesus, He simply responded with Scripture, countering the enemy's temptation with God's truth. If the Word Himself took His stand on the written Word, how much more should we? The Word of God is "...the sword of the Spirit..." (Eph. 6:17). With the sword we can deflect the blows from his deceptive words, as well as attack him. Of all the pieces of armor we are commanded to use, the sword is the only offensive weapon (see Eph. 6:10-18).

That they "...loved not their lives unto the death..." (Rev. 12:11 KJV), is the utter commitment to follow Him regardless of the price. We are called to take up our crosses daily, to do all things for the sake of the gospel, and to no longer live for ourselves but for Him. To the degree that we remain in self-centeredness, we will be vulnerable to the enemy's attack. When we have reckoned ourselves dead to this world, as crucified with Christ, then the enemy no longer has any access to us because he has no more access to Him. If we are dead to this world, what can be done to a dead person? It is impossible for the dead to be offended, to be tempted, to fear, to be depressed, or to be continually looking for the easy way out, because they have already paid the ultimate price.

All of these—the blood of the Lamb, the word of our testimony, and a commitment to lay down our lives—are required for spiritual victory. Anything less will fail to bring a complete victory. We may make occasional, halting advances, but we will sooner or later be pushed back. However, it is clear that at the end of the age an army of believers will be raised up who will not settle for occasional advances—they will have committed themselves to the fight and will not stop until there is the total victory. "The earth is the Lord's, and all it contains..." (Psalm 24:1). Until the earth has been completely recovered from the domain of satan, our fight is not over.

No one will fight to win if they do not believe victory is possible. Many teachings that declare the Church's defeat before Christ's return have been promulgated. Yet the whole prophetic testimony of Scripture is that the Lord, the Church, and the truth are going to prevail. Satan is indeed being cast down to the earth, bringing with him a time of trouble like the world has never known before—but we will still win!

Isaiah 14:16-17 says that when we see satan we are going to marvel at the pitiful nature of the one who caused so much trouble! He who lives within the very least of the saints is much greater than the combined power of all antichrists. These times are not to be feared—this will be our finest hour! As Isaiah 60:1-2 declares, when darkness covers the earth, the glory of the Lord will appear on His people. The darkness will make His glory upon us appear that much brighter. We must start fighting in order to win, giving no more ground to the enemy and taking back what he has usurped.

To effectively combat witchcraft, we must determine that we are going to resist satan until he flees from us. Our goal is more than just driving the enemy out of our own lives; we must also pursue him until he is driven out of others in whom he has established a stronghold. The following are some ways we can combat and overcome eight specific areas of satan's attack through witchcraft.

1. Overcoming Discouragement

Discouragement never comes from God. He is the author of faith and the source of hope which never disappoints. Although God does discipline us when we need it, He never does so by afflicting us with discouragement. When James describes the wisdom that comes from above, he does not list discouragement as one of the characteristics: "But the wisdom from above is first pure, then peaceable, gentle, reasonable, full of mercy and good fruits, unwavering, without hypocrisy" (Jas. 3:17). Discouragement is the very opposite of love, joy, peace, and other attributes of the Holy Spirit's fruit (see Gal. 5:22-23).

We must learn to quickly and instinctively reject discouragement, giving it no place in our thoughts. We must tenaciously resist it, taking every thought captive to obey Christ (see 2 Cor. 10:5). Discouragement must never be allowed to dictate our course. *Faith* is the fruit of the Spirit and the shield of our armor that counters discouragement. If we begin to get discouraged, it is because we have dropped our shield. We need to pick it back up!

2. Overcoming Confusion

"For God is not the author of confusion..." (1 Cor. 14:33 KJV), so we can know for certain that when confusion strikes, it is not coming from Him. In the military, confusion is one of the primary elements of battle that a soldier is trained to handle. Because nothing ever goes exactly as planned, there will rarely be a battle where there is not confusion; the same is true in spiritual warfare.

The disciplined soldier who understands this aspect of warfare learns to use the confusion to his own advantage. He does not let it increase his discouragement, but begins to anticipate it, looking for an opportunity to gain an advantage over the enemy. We must learn to expect confusion as part of the battle and not be surprised or affected by it. Our resolve to stand and fight will quickly dispel this aspect of the attack.

3. Overcoming Depression

God told Cain the most effective remedy for depression:

Then the Lord said to Cain, "Why are you angry? And why has your countenance fallen [the ancient expression for depression]*?*

If you do well, will not your countenance be lifted up? And if you do not do well, sin is crouching at the door; and its desire is for you, but you must master it."

Genesis 4:6-7

Depression is usually the result of allowing discouragement and confusion to cause us to drift from our basic spiritual disciplines, such as reading the Word, praying, fellowshiping, etc. Practicing these disciplines again with resolve will almost always start to reverse the downward spiral.

4. Overcoming a Loss of Vision

This attack can also be turned to our advantage and used as an opportunity. When we begin to lose our vision, we must recommit ourselves to strengthening our vision more than ever. We need to sink our roots deeper, and establish our purpose even more firmly upon the Word of God. When God begins to lead us into a purpose, we should record how He speaks to us. By searching all the Scriptures and reviewing the ways He has led us in the past, we will establish even more firmly His leading.

Above all, we must hold our course! We should not change our direction until we can clearly see the new course. In World War I, one of the most effective tactics of the enemy was to lay a smoke screen in front of allied battleship convoys. As the convoy entered the smoke, visibility was lost. The ships would start turning at any perceived sound or whim, resulting in collisions that sunk more ships than enemy torpedoes did.

The allies finally developed a simple strategy to thwart this tactic against their vision. When in the smoke, every ship was to hold its previous course without deviation. By doing so, they discovered that they would soon sail out the other side into clear air. The same strategy will enable us to more quickly escape whatever is clouding our vision. When we lose our vision, we need to just hold our course and keep moving forward. We will soon break out into the clear.

5. Overcoming Disorientation

As an instrument flight instructor, the first thing I taught each student pilot was that he must not trust his feelings when experiencing restricted visibility while flying on instruments. If a pilot tries to fly by his feelings when in instrument conditions, he will quickly lose control of the plane. Even when flying perfectly straight and level through the clouds, it can begin to feel like the plane is turning. If the pilot reacts to this feeling, he will begin to turn in order to counteract this supposed drift, causing the plane to veer off course or possibly even turning the plane upside down.

In a test conducted by the FAA, a group of pilots without previous instrument training were flown into instrument conditions. Every one of them lost control of their planes because they relied on their feelings for guidance. The same is true of immature Christians who enter spiritual conditions of reduced visibility, or "spiritual clouds." They usually try to rely on their feelings for guidance, and therefore lose control.

The "instruments" we have been given to walk by are found in the Bible. We do not walk by feelings, but by faith in the sure testimony of the Word of God. The Word of God will keep us oriented and on course if we put our trust in it, even when our feelings may tell us to do otherwise.

6. Overcoming Withdrawal

In the Persian Gulf War, the majority of casualties were either reserves or civilians. The safest place to be in the war was on the front line. This has been true in most modern wars, and it is true in spiritual warfare as well.

When you're being pressed in a battle, you cannot call a time-out. On the front line we cannot ask the enemy to stop the battle because we have a headache or want to take a break.

When we are on the front line, we know the dangers and do not let our guard down.

Every Christian is on the front line every day whether he likes it or not. Satan will not stop when we call a time-out. It is when we start to consider ourselves a "civilian," or not a soldier, that we will be the most vulnerable to his attack. A Christian is never in the reserves, but there are times of reprieve from conflict, for seldom do battles continually rage along the entire front. However, when we know we are on the front, even our breaks are taken with vigilance, because we realize that a fresh attack can come at any time. Christians must never remove their spiritual armor or lose their vigilance.

In time of warfare, there are occasions when strategic retreat is necessary. At times, we may overcommit ourselves spiritually and must draw back—but that is not the same as withdrawing from the battle. Even when we overcommit ourselves, retreat should be a last resort because an army in retreat is in its most vulnerable condition. If at all possible, we should at least try to hold our ground until our position can be strengthened.

Even when we discover that in a certain matter we have acted presumptuously, without being commissioned by God, we must not quit—we should repent. There is a difference between quitting and stopping because of repentance. The first is a defeat; the latter is an adjustment that will always result in further victories. Repentance comes because of the truth that sets us free; defeat will result in a spiritual bondage to the power of the enemy.

7. Overcoming Despair

In Genesis 2:18, the Lord said that it was not good for man to be alone. We are social creatures and when we withdraw from fellowship we usually sink into the deepest pit of hopelessness—despair. At this point in the downward spiral, we must return to fellowship and get help in reversing the slide, or else we will be defeated.

As simple as this may seem, *it is the remedy*. Even though fellow believers can be the source of the enemy's attack on us, we must never run away from the Church. We must rather run to it and work out our problems until they are resolved.

8. Overcoming Defeat

Even if satan's stings of witchcraft have brought such devastation to our lives that we are temporarily defeated, we must see that God can still bring us to ultimate victory. Paul commented to the Corinthians that he had been "...struck down, but not destroyed..." (2 Cor. 4:9). At one point, Paul faced such severe attacks that he "...despaired even of life..." (2 Cor. 1:8), but through it all he learned that the secret of regaining victory was not trusting in himself, but in "...God who raised the dead..." (2 Cor. 1:9).

Paul wrote, "...thanks be to God, who gives us victory through our Lord Jesus Christ" (1 Cor. 15:57), and "But in all these things we overwhelmingly conquer through Him who loved us" (Rom. 8:37). Defeat is not an option in Christ. We will gain victory in that which He has called us to do. The only way we can be defeated is to quit.

CHAPTER ELEVEN

COMBATING NEW AGE WITCHCRAFT

THE NEW AGE MOVEMENT IS basically a combination of witchcraft and Hinduism, disguised to make it acceptable to white-collar professionals. There is an important reason why this form of spiritualism is targeting this group. For almost 5,800 years of the earth's 6,000 years of recorded history, nearly 95 percent of all workers were agricultural. In just a little over a century, that statistic has been reversed so that now less than 5 percent of the workers in the West are agricultural. This change has been the result of technological advances. The 5 percent who work in agriculture now produce more than the 95 percent could in the last century.

In the mid 1950s, the number of white-collar workers exceeded the number of blue-collar workers in the West. This majority has grown until it is now estimated that blue-collar workers will go the way of agricultural workers, composing only a very small fraction of the population in the near future. When it was predicted that "...knowledge will increase" (Dan. 12:4) in the end times, few could have comprehended the degree to which this would happen. Information is now the most valuable commodity in the world, and the job of accumulating, interpreting, packaging, and transferring knowledge has become the world's largest industry.

Those involved in the knowledge industry are not only the most numerous, they are also the wealthiest and most powerful. They are also a group that the Church has become increasingly unsuccessful in reaching, which has also made them an appealing target for the New Age movement and other cults. Because man was created to have fellowship with God, who is Spirit, there is a spiritual void in man that hungers for the supernatural.

The day of supernatural neutrality is over. Those who do not know the true supernatural power of God will become increasingly subject to the evil and counterfeit supernatural powers of the enemy. Those whose doctrines or fears have led them to avoid the supernatural power of God will find themselves, and especially their children, easy prey to evil, supernatural power.

KINGDOMS IN CONFLICT

Paul explained, "For the kingdom of God does not consist in words but in power" (1 Cor. 4:20). Satan knows this, and is therefore quite content to fight the battle on the level of words and doctrines. Regardless of how accurately we can argue doctrinal positions, satan will have little problem conquering us if we do not know the power of God, which is a fundamental aspect of God's Kingdom. Those who really believe the Bible will walk in power. Righteousness is the result of believing in our hearts, not just in our minds, and those who do not know the power of God are only believing in Him in their minds.

Considering the foolish antics of those who have known the power of God in the Pentecostal, charismatic, full gospel, and third wave movements, it is easy to understand why many would shy away from the gifts of the Spirit. But this too is one of the tests that separate the true believers from those who only know creeds or doctrines—God has made the foolish things of the world to confound the wise. Only the humble will be involved in what He is doing, and He will give His grace only to them.

Churches that have rejected the supernatural power of God have become increasingly irrelevant and unable to reach the world, for the battle for men's souls is intensely supernatural in nature. The more secularized society becomes, the more it actually magnifies people's hunger for the super-natural. Hence, atheists tend to be drawn to the most base forms of witchcraft and the black arts, which they are deceived into thinking are powers resident within man, when actually these powers are demonic in nature.

The denominations and movements within the Church that have rejected the power of God are almost all shrinking, because they have become irrelevant and boring, with little or no power to attract converts. Many churches and denominations that have rejected the power of God have already succumbed to influences from the New Age movement. Others are succumbing to the spirit of the age in other forms, not only tolerating the perverted and unbelievers as members, but actually ordaining them as pastors and leaders. Contrary to this, the denominations and movements that preach and walk in the supernatural power of God are not only growing, but are by far the fastest growing religious movements in the world. Paul the apostle declared:

*And my message and my preaching were not in persuasive
words of wisdom, but in demonstration of the Spirit and of
power,*

*so that your faith would not rest on the wisdom of men, but
on the power of God.*

1 Corinthians 2:4-5

The conflict between the Kingdom of God and the
kingdom of evil is not just a conflict between truth and error,
but a confrontation of supernatural powers, with both sides
seeking to fill the spiritual void in man created by the Fall.

The entire history of God's dealings with mankind have
involved demonstrations of supernatural power. It is incon-
gruous to say we are a biblical people and yet not walk in the
supernatural power of God. True Christianity is not just a
matter of words; it is a demonstration of God's love and power
to save, heal, and deliver. Jesus stated that as the Father had
sent Him into the world, He has sent us into the world (see Jn.
17:18). As our example, Jesus did not just talk about God's
power to heal and save, He demonstrated it.

If we are going to preach the gospel, we must preach it as He
did, demonstrating both God's love and power. When Jesus sent
out His disciples to preach the Kingdom, they were to heal the
sick and cast out demons (see Lk. 9:1-2). The Lord never changes
nor does He change the way He sends His true messengers.

Many biblical prophecies concerning the end of the age
address the supernatural nature of the conflicts that will occur.
A church that does not walk in God's power will become
increasingly inadequate to deal with the times and confront the
powers that come against it. To overcome the increasing power
of the enemy we must "...desire earnestly spiritual gifts, but
especially that you may prophesy" (1 Cor. 14:1). "God is spirit,

and those who worship Him must worship in spirit and truth" (Jn. 4:24). Again, the first defense against the deceptive supernatural power of the enemy is to know the true power of God.

Most believers have *some* desire for spiritual gifts, but we must *"earnestly"* desire them if we are going to receive them. Even though most of the Church is now "open" for God to use them in a demonstration of His power, He has decreed that we must *ask, seek,* and *knock* in order to receive (see Mt. 7:7). Those who are just "open" for the Lord to use them are rarely used. Being "open" is usually a cop-out for those who are either too fearful or too prideful to risk failure. It takes faith and persistent seeking if we are to receive.

PIOUS DELUSIONS

It is often repeated that we are to seek the Giver and not the gifts. That sounds pious, but it is not biblical. Certainly we are to seek the Giver more than the gifts, but we are commanded to seek the gifts too. The two are not mutually exclusive. Seeking to walk in the gifts of the Spirit is actually one form of seeking God, and even more important, it is being obedient. Many such glib statements of apparent wisdom are merely human wisdom and often in conflict with the Scriptures.

Our God is supernatural and we cannot truly desire fellowship with Him without desiring fellowship with the supernatural. While many Christians have been hardened by doctrines that justify their powerlessness, claiming that God no longer moves supernaturally, even those believers long in their hearts for the supernatural. We were all created for fellowship in the Spirit, which is by definition supernatural.

Recently, some of the world's most brilliant theologians and apologists, who believed God no longer worked supernaturally, have been won over and are now walking in God's power themselves, often after witnessing just one genuine miracle. Genuine is the key word here. Those who sincerely love God and seek to walk in His power are turned off by the fakery and hype often associated with the ministries of those who really do not yet have God's power.

THE TRUE GOSPEL

True Christianity is the true Word of God verified by the true power of God. Jesus went about to "do and teach" (Acts 1:1). He usually performed miracles *before* He taught. He knew that people who had an undeniable encounter with God would be far more open to what He said to them. The power Jesus and His apostles demonstrated was used to confirm and illuminate their teachings.

The same is still true. The demonstration of God's power transforms intellectual concepts into a true faith in the teachings of the Lord. It takes both the Word and the power of God to change the inner man. Without both, we may change our outward behavior, but our hearts remain untouched. It is the spiritual void in the heart that must be filled by a true fellowship with God if we are going to be free from the spiritual influence and power of the enemy.

Because witchcraft is counterfeit spiritual authority, we will only be completely free from the power of witchcraft when we are completely submitted to the authority of God. If the spiritual void that is in us is not filled with the real power and authority of God, we will become subject to witchcraft in some form as we draw closer to the end of the age. The Battle of Armageddon is fought in the "valley of decision" (Joel 3:14);

everyone on earth will be brought to the place of making a decision. It is a power confrontation, and the choice will be made concerning issues of power and authority. We will choose either the power and authority of God, or the power and authority of the evil one—but we will all choose.

DISCERNING COUNTERFEITS

All of the spiritual gifts available to the Church are presently being counterfeited by the enemy. Ironically, those whose lack of faith causes them to avoid spiritual gifts in order to keep from being deceived, are *certain* to be deceived. We must walk by faith, not fear, if we are going to stay on the path that leads to life. Fear will inevitably lead us to deception if we allow it to be our motivation.

If we are going to fulfill the purpose of God, it will take a faith like Abraham's, willing to risk leaving everything behind in order to seek that which He is building. If we are going to walk in the power of God, we must have more faith in God to lead us into all truth than we do in the enemy's ability to deceive us. Faith is the door to fellowship with God, because it takes faith to reach beyond the natural realm to the supernatural so that we can see Him who is unseen.

As we walk in faith, what we begin to see with the eyes of our hearts will become more real to us than what we are seeing with our natural eyes. Then we will begin living more for the eternal than for the temporal. Those who walk in true faith are naturally going to appear foolish to those who live according to the wisdom of this world, or those who are of a "natural mind."

We take a major step in being delivered from the power of witchcraft when we start to see the Lord so clearly that we respect and serve Him more than anything else. Then we are no longer subject to the influence, manipulation, and control of those who are still earthly minded, or who move in the power of witchcraft.

Those who give themselves to becoming authorities on the nature of evil almost always become darkened and evil in nature themselves. Many "cult watchers" have released a more foul spirit in the Church than the cults they were watching. The paranoia they have promulgated has done more to bring division and damage to the Church than any cult has been able to do. These people have often become the "fault finders" that Jude talked about, printing and distributing slander and gossip as if it were researched fact. As Jude warned, these are being reserved for the "black darkness" (see Jude 10-16), in which many of them have already begun to live.

We do not need to study the darkness as much as we need to study the light. Light will always overpower darkness. If we walk in the light, we will cast out the darkness. If we walk in the true supernatural power of God, we will overpower the evil supernatural power as surely as Moses confounded the sorcerers of Egypt. But Moses would not have been successful had he gone to Egypt with no power, and neither will we succeed in setting people free today if we are powerless. The increasing power of the enemy will not be effectively con-fronted and driven out without the power of God.

THE ENEMY'S STRATEGY

Most cults and New Age groups are now blatantly attacking Christianity, focusing on the Church as the main target of their sorcery. Not only are they infiltrating the Church, but they are using their power to cast spells on those in ministry. In my book *The Harvest*, I wrote of cult members en-tering church meetings and performing lewd acts to intimidate and humiliate believers and this has already begun to happen with alarming frequency.

There is a simple solution for churches that have become the target of such attacks—they must seek to know and walk in God's authority and power. He who is in us is much greater than he who is in the world (see 1 John 4:4). As the Church grows in true spiritual authority, the cults are going to fear us far more than we fear them.

Sorcerers usually try to avoid direct confrontation with those who have true spiritual authority. Although they will attack those who are growing in spiritual authority and bearing fruit for the Kingdom of God, this is generally not done openly, but in secret. The attacks are done indirectly by sacrificing and cursing according to the black arts.

We must recognize the power in satanic sacrifices if we are going to overcome them. In 2 Kings 3:27, the king of Moab offered his oldest son as a burnt offering to his demon gods and as a result, "...there came great wrath against Israel, and they departed..." (from attacking Moab). It is not biblical for a Christian to fear the enemy, but if we do not understand and properly respect his power, we will be vulnerable to his influence.

When combating evil powers we cannot rely on carnal weapons or mere human strength—neither can we fight on satan's terms. His first strategy in a confrontation is to get us out of the Holy Spirit's control and into a spirit of retaliation. We cannot overcome evil with evil; satan will not cast out satan. Jesus said, "But if I cast out demons by the Spirit of God, then the kingdom of God has come upon you" (Mt. 12:28).

This is why Jesus commanded us to "bless those who curse you..." (Lk. 6:28). Blessings are more powerful than any curse, and will quickly overcome them. Even so, it is important for us to recognize when we are being cursed with witchcraft, so that we can defend against it and shine light into the darkness that has been directed against us.

Summary

Witchcraft is basically the practice of cursing others. This cursing does not just come through cults or black magic arts, but can even come through those who love us and have good intentions, but who are trying to manipulate us. Using manipulation or a control spirit is a form or witchcraft, regardless of who does it.

The mother who manipulates her son or daughter into marrying *her* choice has done it through witchcraft, and such relationships usually have to be held together through continued manipulation and control. The prayer group who uses prayers to expose the sins of others is gossiping for the sake of manipulation. This is not genuine prayer—it is witchcraft. Much of what is written in the name of Christian journalism purportedly as an attempt to keep the Church informed is gossip, used to manipulate or gain influence over others—this too is witchcraft.

When spiritual leaders use manipulation, hype, or control to build their churches or ministries, they are operating in a counterfeit spiritual authority equivalent to witchcraft. Much of what is taught in business schools is a form of manipulation or control that is witchcraft. Many of the strategies the Church has borrowed from secular journalism and the business world have brought witchcraft into the camp, and it must be removed if we are to be free to accomplish our purpose for this hour.

Many of the "yokes" and human expectations that we face have some power of manipulation and witchcraft attached to them. The enemy wants to establish these strongholds to conflict with the calling of God in our lives. However, this is not a license to disregard the expectations of our parents, teachers, employers, etc. We were known by the Lord before we were born, and many of the influences in our lives have been placed there to help steer us toward our purposes in Him. But some of the yokes and expectations that well-intentioned parents, teachers, or coaches place upon us must be cast off. When yokes are placed upon us that are not from the Lord, they will become clear as we come to know our calling and purpose in Him because the truth will set us free.

The only yoke that we must take is the Lord's yoke. His yoke is easy and His burden is light (see Mt. 11:28-30). When we take His yoke we find rest and refreshment instead of the pressure and discouragement that comes from "white" witchcraft. Pressure tactics and manipulation are subtle forms of witchcraft that can have just as much power as the black magic arts. White and black witchcraft may be different branches but they have the same root and the same deadly poison.

Unfortunately, even when unstable people recognize the dangers of being subject to charismatic or "white" witchcraft, they will often distort this principle in order to rebel against God's ordained authority over their lives. King Saul is the personification of one who was ordained by God but fell from his place of true spiritual authority to operate in counterfeit spiritual authority. King David, on the other hand, is a personification of true spiritual authority. How did David react to Saul? He was willing to serve in the house of Saul until Saul chased him away. Even then he never retaliated, rebelled, or tried to undermine Saul's authority, but chose instead to honor him as "the Lord's anointed" (1 Sam. 24:10).

We need to learn from David's example. Even though he was called to take Saul's place, he never lifted his hand against Saul. David determined that if God had really called him to be the next king then God would have to be the one to establish him. David overcame evil with good by demonstrating the exact opposite of the manipulative or control spirits that had come against him. Had David manipulated his way into the kingdom, he would have almost certainly fallen to witchcraft just like Saul. But David was of a different spirit.

Those who are the target of any form of witchcraft will usually feel the sequence of stings previously listed. If we react to the attack properly, we will not only be free of its influence ourselves, but we can also help to free those who have used witchcraft. The manipulation and control spirits gain entrance through fear. Those who are fearful and insecure are so obsessed with controlling others that they use evil influence, and it will take a demonstration of "perfect love" (see 1 Jn. 4:18) to cast out these fears. Jesus commanded us to "bless those who curse you" (see Mt. 5:44 NKJV). Paul said that we are not to return evil for evil; we are to overcome evil with good (see Rom. 12:19-21).

When we discover that we are the target of witchcraft, retaliation is not the answer. In fact, that is the very thing the enemy would have us do, for it multiplies the evil we are trying to cast out. Satan will not cast out satan; witchcraft will not cast out witchcraft. We must pray for those who are praying against us and bless those who are cursing us. This does not mean we are to bless what they are *doing*, but we must pray that they are delivered from the fears and hatred that motivate them. Pray for your attackers to have a revelation of the perfect love of God. Our greatest victory is in winning those who are in the enemy's grip, not afflicting them in retaliation.

There is another source of witchcraft that can be one of the most unexpected causes of our discouragement, confusion, depression, loss of vision, disorientation, and despair— ourselves! When we use manipulation, hype, or control on others, we open ourselves to the consequences. Before we look at others to find the source, we should first look at ourselves. Again, satan cannot cast out satan; we will not be able to cast witchcraft out of others if we are using it ourselves.

Most who have been subject to witchcraft have tried to combat it in the flesh, actually using the same spirit. When we do that, it gains a foothold in our own lives that must be broken before we will have the authority to deliver others.

Witchcraft is a serious offense that God will not continue to tolerate in the Church. His intent is to bring down every form and manifestation of witchcraft that ensnares His people. After we have been freed from this terrible evil, we will also be free to walk in the unprecedented power He will entrust to those who walk in true spiritual authority.

Chapter Twelve

Witchcraft
in the Media

In one of the most remarkable statements made in the New Testament, Peter wrote that we should be "looking for and hastening the coming of the day of God..." (2 Pet. 3:12). Obviously, Peter would not have said this if it were not *possible* for us to hasten the coming of the day of God. But if we can hasten the coming of His day, it is apparent that we can also *delay* it. Because the enemy knows his time is short, we can be sure that he is doing all that he can to keep us from moving in what will hasten the day of the Lord and to also cause its delay.

The harvest will come. It has already come to many parts of the world. However, there are major stumbling blocks to spiritual advancement that we must address if we are going to receive the full benefit of the impending awakening. These stumbling blocks are not powerful enough to stop revival altogether, but they can limit its scope, depth, duration, and fruit.

The harvest will bring the reaping of everything that has been sown, both good and evil. The harvest that marks the end of this age has already begun, but because many have the concept that the harvest is only a great revival, they do not see it or understand it. The Scriptures teach that the harvest will begin with the tares being taken out first (see Mt. 13:38-40,49), and this has been happening for some time. In many ways it seems that we have *only* been reaping tares. This has been painful for a season, but the pain will be appreciated when the full harvest begins and we are able to avoid repeating the same mistakes.

One aspect of the harvest of tares that had a significant impact on the international Body of Christ came with the televangelist scandals of recent years. This is not to imply that the individuals involved were "tares"; more importantly the scandals that were brought to light began to uproot some erroneous practices and theologies. Unfortunately, these tares were not exposed by the Church, but by the secular news media. As a friend remarked in a roundtable meeting that we hosted, "The Lord is using the secular media to discipline the Church because we have refused to judge ourselves." There is an important truth to this observation.

That the Lord is using the secular media to discipline the Church is a loud signal announcing our fallen condition. It is likewise apparent that much of the Church has sincerely given herself to repentance. A sign that this repentance has been genuine enough to be acceptable to God will be when our sovereignty is restored, and when the Church is able to judge herself.

Even though the Lord used the heathen nations to discipline Israel for her apostasies, afterward He often destroyed those nations for their arrogance. This may shock our human sensibilities, but those heathen nations were still heathen. They still worshiped idols and would inevitably try to introduce their idol worship to Israel during their occupation.

The same has been happening between the secular media and the Church. Much of the Christian media has been turning to the ways of the secular media. This is not the means by which the Lord intended to discipline the Church, and it will result in even worse consequences if we do not rid ourselves of it.

THE WRONG KIND OF REPENTANCE

In general, journalism has crossed a line that has made it one of the primary platforms of the "accuser of our brethren" (see Rev. 12:10). Of course, there are some journalists whom this would not apply to, but the foundational principles of modern journalism have married it more to Greek philosophy than to Christianity. Unfortunately, this is also the philosophy that most "Christian" journalists operate by. In fact, the Christian media has at times proven even less honorable and truthful in its reporting than the secular media, causing it to become a major stumbling block to spiritual advancement.

The Christian media is now founded more upon a humanistic philosophy of journalism than upon biblical principles. Today the Christian media is one of the greatest sources of deadly poison that is spreading destruction in the Western Church, through the spirit of *unrighteous judgment.* Although the Lord may have used the media because we would not judge ourselves, the solution is not for us to take on the ways of the heathen, but to return to God's righteous judgment as outlined in His Word.

There is healthy skepticism that truly *wants* to believe, as the Bereans did when they searched the Scriptures to verify the message of Paul and Barnabas. However, there is another kind of skeptic who only wants to *doubt.* This unhealthy form of skepticism wants to see the worst in others, because that somehow makes the skeptic look bigger or at least feel better about his own flaws.

This kind of doubt and cynicism is both tragic and deadly. When the chronicles of this earth are read on that great judgment day, we will probably learn that this evil form of doubt was far more deadly than cancer or AIDS. Great souls rise to even greater heights by lifting others higher. Criticism has an appearance of wisdom, but it is wisdom from the dark side, and it is the fruit of the Tree of the Knowledge of Good and Evil.

Since the 1960s, the news media of the West, including the Christian media, seems to have been almost completely taken over by this dark side of skepticism. It is now almost unthinkable for a Christian journalist to write an article about a church, movement, or event, without at least throwing in some criticism. This is often done by reporting hearsay or crude gossip as fact, without even contacting the offended parties for their side of the story.

Those who simply pass on gossip are just as guilty of gossiping as those who originated it. All of this is usually done in the name of "the people's right to know," or "to protect people from error." However, are we really protecting them from error when we do so by committing one of the most serious errors of all—becoming stumbling blocks?

The Scriptures are shockingly honest about exposing both the good qualities and the flaws in even the greatest spiritual heroes. Yet the Bible was written as history for the sake of instructing others in the ways of God, not for the sake of exposing dirt. How does today's Christian journalism justify its departure from such biblical exhortations as these:

*Let **no unwholesome word** proceed from your mouth, but only such a word as is good for edification according to the need of the moment, that it may give **grace** to those who hear.*

Ephesians 4:29

And your brother sins, go and reprove him in private....

Matthew 18:15

In Matthew 18, the procedure for addressing sin was given to keep us from becoming stumbling blocks. Not following this procedure, especially in journalism, may have created more stumbling blocks to the Lord's own children than any other source. Much more damage has probably come to the Church by such journalism, and by so-called heresy hunting, than has come through the heresies they are trying to expose.

By What Authority?

In his June 8, 1978 commencement address at Harvard University, Alexander Solzhenitsyn said, "Such as it is, however, the press has become the greatest power within the Western countries, more powerful than the legislature, the executive, and the judiciary. One would then like to ask: By what law has it been elected and to whom is it responsible?" Solzhenitsyn's question is valid for Western society, but even more so for the Church.

On what basis has the press been granted the extra-ordinary power it now has? By what authority has it been elected? The Lord appoints elders in the Church to give it both protection and direction. He has set high standards for those elders who would be given such influence. In contrast, to whom are the Christian journalists accountable, and to what standards must they be held? These are important questions.

Just as the secular media can now manipulate public opinion and dictate policy, sometimes even more effectively than our elected officials, Christian journalists can do the same in the Church. Who gave them this power? Is it derived merely from an ability to be articulate or because of the anointing and commission of God? Do we have the right to exert a massive influence in the Church simply because we have the marketing ability to distribute our magazines, newsletters, or programs?

James warned, "Let not many of you become teachers, my brethren, knowing that as such we will incur a stricter judgment" (Jas. 3:1). It is a most serious matter to have influence in the Lord's own household! Let us be very careful how we attain it, and how we use it.

Paul explained that he did not presume to go beyond the sphere of authority that was appointed to him (see 2 Cor. 10:14-18). He realized that God has given each of us certain realms of authority and grace, and we need to take care that we don't go beyond these appointed realms.

WHERE ARE THE ELDERS?

Much of what is done today by Christian journalism, and the heresy hunters, encroaches upon the realm of authority that was given to the elders of the Church. The very meaning of the word *elder* implies a certain degree of longevity in faithful service to the Church before one is given this influence. The position of elder is the highest and most respected office appointed in the biblical Church.

Journalists today, on the other hand, are often not accountable to anyone. Even though they are not required to comply with any of the biblical standards for leadership in the Church, they can have more influence through the media than even the most anointed true elders.

Writing can be an aspect of a biblical ministry and there are journalists who have obvious spiritual ministries as teachers, pastors, etc. Some of these have been faithful to the biblical standards required for leaders in the Church, and they should be recognized as elders in the Body of Christ. For such people, journalism can be a proper platform for the authority they have been given by God. Even so, they too can become stumbling blocks if they do not comply with the biblical procedures for bringing correction in the Church.

Most who are sources of the prevailing critical spirit or spirit of unrighteous judgment are those who are not standing on true anointing, but on a platform of influence gained by other means. Some received their position because of professional training, which came from schools founded upon a humanistic philosophy of journalism. This philosophy does have the appearance of wisdom and the search for truth, but is actually in conflict with the Truth Himself. Others may have been given a true commission from God, but have compromised with the spirit of the world.

John said, "...the whole world lies in the power of the evil one" (1 Jn. 5:19). The ways of the world are not the ways of God and as Paul exhorted the Ephesians:

> ...in reference to your former manner of life, you lay aside the old self, which is being corrupted in accordance with the lusts of deceit,
>
> and that you be renewed in the spirit of your mind,

and put on the new self, which in the likeness of God has
been created in righteousness and holiness of the truth.

Ephesians 4:22-24

If we're going to be "created in righteousness and holiness of the truth," we must put on a new self, and live by a different philosophy than that of the world.

GOOD INTENTIONS

Many Christian journalists entered the field with the intention of trying to provide an alternative source of information to the secular media. This is a noble vision and is truly needed. The Church is called to be the pillar and support of the truth. However, the accuracy level of reporting in Christian journalism has not proven to be any higher than in secular journalism—it only has a more "spiritual" slant to it.

The investigative reporting done by Christian journalists on the events that I have personally witnessed, or about the people I know, has been shockingly dishonest and untrue. Some were so prone to the use of gossip, hearsay, or even apparent imagination that they could rival some of the grocery counter tabloids. Truth is our most precious commodity, and we cannot continue to allow it to be compromised or we will receive the judgment that is promised for such deception.

In an article printed in a Christian magazine about myself and our ministry, we struggled to find a single fact that was accurate. Even the positive things they had to say were distorted to the degree that we had a hard time understanding what they were talking about. When we tried to find out how it had gotten so far off track, it became obvious that their research was as flawed as the tabloids. Anything labeled Christian should have integrity that greatly exceeds the world's standards, not falls to their lowest level.

I went to the owner of this magazine and he listened patiently, but never once acknowledged a mistake. I never felt any malice on his or the writer's part. A drunken driver may not have any malice in his heart toward the people that he kills, but they are just as dead. Carelessness kills, and drunken driving kills more people than murderers do each year. The media is intoxicated right now with its own power and influence, and they are hurting a lot of people with their drunken carelessness.

Those who have been influenced by the humanistic philosophy of journalism may think we are shallow, blind, or duped if we do not expose the wrongs of others when we write about them. Yet it is much better to be ridiculed by men than it is for God to think of us as stumbling blocks. We all must stand in front of the judgment seat of Christ, and those who are trying to sit in it now without authority will have a most difficult time on that day.

The world's methods for seeking truth are very different from the way that real truth is found. Truth is only found in Jesus, and can only be found when we are being led by the Holy Spirit. Secular schools may be able to teach us something about the mechanics of writing or the technical knowledge needed to understand today's media tools, but the philosophy that is sown into their students is devastating when incorporated into Christian media.

JUDGMENT ON JOURNALISM

Christian television ministries have come under severe judgment in the last few years. Television has vastly given more influence to some people in the Church than God ever intended them to have. Whenever we move beyond the sphere of authority that has been appointed to us by God, we have moved beyond grace and we are bound to fall.

Other forms of Christian media are about to experience the same scrutiny that the television ministries have undergone. The Lord will ultimately deal with the secular media as well, but "...it is time for judgment to begin with the household of God..." (1 Pet. 4:17). Christian journalism will soon come under the same kind of judgment that television ministries have been experiencing.

For a period of time, the public's trust and esteem of televangelists probably sank lower than that of any other professional group, including politicians and lawyers. There are, of course, politicians and lawyers who live their lives by the highest standards of integrity and they too must bear the judgment of their profession because there are fundamental roots in these professions that must be corrected. There are likewise many journalists who sincerely attempt to live by the highest standards of truth and integrity, but they are often trying to do so on a foundation that simply will not support the truth. That is why the very foundations are being shaken, so only that which cannot be shaken will remain (see Heb. 12:25-28).

We will soon enter a period when Christian magazines, journals, newsletters, and newspapers will all come under the most intense pressure and scrutiny. The exposers are about to be exposed, and they will receive back the same measure of judgment that they measured out to others. Even those who have tried to be honest and fair, but have been operating on a humanistic foundation, will see their faulty foundations collapse.

Can this judgment be avoided? The Scriptures clearly teach that judgment can be avoided by genuine repentance. As

Paul told the Corinthians, "If we judged ourselves rightly, we should not be judged" (1 Cor. 11:31). Repentance is more than requesting forgiveness for our wrongs—repentance is going back to where we missed the turn and getting back on the right road. It also often includes restitution for the wrongs that have caused injury to others.

We must remember that the harvest is the reaping of what has been sown, and, "...in the way you judge, you will be judged; and by your standard of measure, it will be measured to you" (Mt. 7:2). If we have sown unrighteous judgments, then judgment will soon come upon us. If we want to reap grace, however, we should use every opportunity that we can to sow grace. If we desire to reap mercy, we must use every opportunity to sow mercy. "Do not be deceived, God is not mocked; for whatever a man sows, this he will also reap" (Gal. 6:7).

The Grace of True Authority

According to the many examples in the New Testament, there are times when the errors of certain movements or sects must be addressed. The Lord Himself warned His disciples, saying, "...beware of the leaven of the Pharisees..." (Mt. 16:6). Major portions of the Book of Galatians and other apostolic letters are devoted to correcting mistakes in doctrine or practice. The main difference between these scriptural examples and what is so often done today is that the biblical writers had the *authority* to bring the needed correction.

One reason there is so much wrong judgment, or needed correction that is given in the wrong spirit or manner, is the vacuum that exists because those who truly have been given authority by God have refrained from using it. This does not justify the wrong use of authority, or the presumption of those who try to bring correction to the Church without having the authority, but it does make such actions more understandable. We can even appreciate the courage that some have shown by addressing issues that no one else would address, but that still does not make it right. Even worse, it puts those courageous people in jeopardy of becoming stumbling blocks. Paul's lament to the Corinthians still applies to the Church today:

> *Or do you not know that the saints will judge the world? If the world is judged by you, are you not competent to constitute the smallest law courts?*
>
> *Do you not know that we shall judge angels? How much more, matters of this life?*
>
> 1 Corinthians 6:2-3

Possibly the main reason that the Church is so full of unrighteous judgment is because there is no format for *righteous* judgment in the Church. Until the elders take their proper places in the gates, churches will continue to be subject to the judgment of the secular media and heresy hunters. Regardless of how well-intentioned they may be, division and unrighteous judgment are sown which wound the Body of Christ more than rectify the errors they seek to expose.

The Lord has given mandates to the Church that we cannot accomplish without unity. Righteous judgment is one of them. This issue must be addressed by Church leaders on every level if we are going to accomplish our mandate for this hour. Unrighteous judgment is a source of most of the conflicts in the world. Since the Church is called to be the light of this world, we should have the answers to the world's problems. But how can we help to bring righteous judgment to the world if we cannot even judge ourselves?

Because of the many excesses of the past or the tendency of some to presume authority beyond their appointed jurisdiction, it is easy to understand why we tend to shy away from this difficult issue. However, because of our continued neglect of this basic mandate—to provide righteous judgment to the Church, and then through the Church to ourselves, we will continue to be subject to the unrighteous judgment of the world.

PART THREE

THE RELIGIOUS SPIRIT

Chapter Thirteen

Understanding the Religious Spirit

Loving God is the greatest commandment and the greatest gift that we can receive. The second greatest commandment is to love our neighbors. As the Lord affirmed, the whole law is fulfilled by keeping these two commandments. That means, if we keep these two commandments we will keep the whole law (see Mt. 22:34-40; Rom. 13:8). If we love the Lord, we will not worship idols, and if we love our neighbors we will not envy them, steal from them, murder them, etc. Therefore, keeping these two positive commandments to love will enable us to obey all of the negative "do nots" of the law.

Simple love for God will overcome most of the evil in our hearts, and it is the most powerful weapon against evil in the world. Because loving God is our highest goal, it must be the primary focus of our lives. To divert us from this ultimate quest, the enemy uses one of his most deceptive and deadly attacks upon the Church through the religious spirit. The devil wants to keep us focused on the evil in our lives knowing that we will become what we are beholding (see 2 Cor. 3:18). As long as we keep looking at the evil it will continue to have dominion over us. On the contrary, when we look to the Lord and behold His glory, we will be changed into His image.

This is not to imply that we should ignore the sins and errors that are in our lives. In fact, the Scriptures command us to examine ourselves and test ourselves to be sure that we are still in the faith (see 2 Cor. 13:5). The issue is what we do after the iniquity is discovered. Do we turn to the Tree of the Knowledge of Good and Evil, or to the Tree of Life? Do we try to make ourselves better so that we will then be acceptable to God or do we turn to the cross of Jesus to find both forgiveness and power to overcome the sin?

A primary strategy of the enemy is intended to keep us focused on the evil, partaking of the Tree of Knowledge and away from the glory of the Lord and the cross. This tactic comes in the form of a religious spirit, an evil spirit that is the counterfeit of the true love of God and true worship. This guise for true religion has probably done far more damage to the Church than the New Age movement and all other cults combined.

THE NATURE OF A RELIGIOUS SPIRIT

A religious spirit is a demon that seeks to substitute religious activity for the power of the Holy Spirit in our lives. Its primary objective is to have the Church "holding to a form of godliness, although they have denied its power..." (2 Tim. 3:5). The apostle Paul completed his exhortation with "*avoid* such men as these." This religious spirit is the "...leaven of the Pharisees and Sadducees" (Mt. 16:6) of which the Lord warned His disciples to beware.

The Lord often used metaphors to illustrate the lessons He taught. The religious spirit operates like the leaven in bread, which does not add substance or nutritional value to the bread—it only inflates it. Such is the by-product of the religious spirit. It does not add to the life or power of the Church, it merely feeds the very pride of man which caused the first fall and almost every fall since.

Satan seems to understand even better than the Church that "...God resists the proud, but gives grace to the humble..." (Jas. 4:6 NKJV). He knows very well that God will not inhabit any work that is inflated with pride, and that God Himself will even resist such a work. So Satan's strategy is to make us proud—even proud of good things, such as how much we read our Bibles, or witness, or feed the poor. He knows that if we do the will of God in pride, our work will be counterproductive and could even ultimately work toward our fall.

Satan also knows that once leaven gets into the bread, it is extremely difficult to remove. Pride, by its very nature, is the most difficult stronghold to remove or correct. A religious spirit keeps us from hearing the voice of God by encouraging us to assume that we already know God's opinion, what He is saying, and what pleases Him. This delusion is the result of believing that God is just like us. A religious spirit encourages the rationalization of Scripture, having us believe that rebukes, exhortations, and words of correction are for other people, but not for us.

If a religious spirit is a problem in your life, you have probably already begun to think about how badly someone you know needs to read this chapter. It may not even have occurred to you that God put this book into your hands because you need it. In fact, we all need it. This is one enemy that all of us

131

are battling to some degree. It is imperative that we get free of this devastating deception and stay free. We will not be able to worship the Lord in Spirit and truth until we do.

The degree to which we have been delivered from this powerful deception will directly affect the degree to which we are able to preach the true gospel in power. The Church's confrontation with the religious spirit will be one of the epic battles of the last days. Everyone will be fighting in this battle. The only issue to be determined is which side we are on.

We will never have the authority to deliver others from darkness until we are free from it ourselves. To begin taking ground from this vast enemy, we must ask the Lord to shine His light on us, showing how this applies to us personally. As illustrated by the Lord's continual confrontations with the Pharisees, the Church's most desperate fight from the very beginning has been with this spirit. Just as the primary characteristic of the Pharisees was focusing on what was wrong with others while being blind to their own faults, the religious spirit tries to make us do the same.

THE GREAT DECEPTION

One of the most deceptive characteristics about the religious spirit is that it is founded upon zeal for God. We tend to think that zeal for God could only be good, but we need to consider *why* we are zealous for Him.

Paul wrote of his Jewish brethren in Romans 10:2: "For I bear witness that they have a *zeal* for God, but not in accordance with knowledge." No one on earth prayed more, fasted more, read the Bible more, had a greater hope in the coming of the Messiah, or had more zeal for the things of God than the Pharisees. Yet, they were the greatest opposers of God and His Messiah when He came.

The young Saul of Tarsus was motivated by zeal for God while he was persecuting His Church. Zeal for God is one of the most desperately needed characteristics of the Church today, most of which is bound by a terrible Laodicean lukewarmness. The Lord commanded the Laodicean Church to "...be zealous, therefore, and repent" (Rev. 3:19).

Those who are truly zealous are the most difficult to stop, so the enemy's strategy against them is to push them too far. His first step is to persuade them to glory in their own zeal. Regardless of how important our characteristics or gifts may be, if the enemy can get us to take pride in them, he will have caught us in his snare and they will be used for evil.

The Lord had little trouble with demons while He walked the earth. They quickly recognized His authority and begged for mercy. It was the conservative, zealous, religious community that immediately became His greatest enemy. Those who were the most zealous for the Word of God crucified the Word Himself when He became flesh to walk among them. The same is still true.

All of the cults and false religions combined have not done as much damage to the moves of God as the opposition, or infiltration, of the religious spirit in the Church. Cults and false religions are easily discerned, but the religious spirit has thwarted or diverted possibly every revival or movement to date, and it still retains a seat of honor throughout most of the visible Church.

It is a manifestation of the religious spirit that will take its seat in the very temple of God, declaring himself to be God (2 Thess. 2:4). The temple of God is no longer made with hands, and this is not speaking about a building in Jerusalem.

This man of sin will take his seat *in the Church.* Unfortunately, it will be the Church that allows him to do so.

THE TWO FOUNDATIONS

Like most of the enemy's strongholds, the religious spirit builds its work on two basic foundations: fear and pride. *The religious spirit seeks to have us serve the Lord in order to gain His approval, rather than receiving approval through the cross of Jesus.* Therefore, the religious spirit bases relationship to God on personal discipline rather than the propitiatory sacrifice of Christ. The motivation for doing this can be fear or pride, or a combination of both.

Fear and pride are the two basic results of the Fall, and our deliverance from them is usually a long process, which is why the Lord even gave Jezebel "time to repent" (see Rev. 2:20-21). The biblical Jezebel, the wife of King Ahab, was a very religious woman, but she was given to false religion. The Lord gave her time to repent, because the roots of this spirit go so deep that time is required to fully repent and be delivered from it.

However, even though the Lord gave Jezebel time to repent, He rebuked the church of Thyatira for *tolerating* her (see v. 20). We can be patient with people who have religious spirits, but we must not tolerate their ministry in our midst while we are waiting! If this spirit is not confronted quickly, it will possibly do more damage to the Church, our ministries, our families, and our lives, than any other assault that we may suffer.

THE FOUNDATION OF GUILT

Eli, the priest who raised the prophet Samuel, is a biblical example of someone who ministered in a religious spirit founded upon guilt. Eli had so much zeal for the Lord that when he heard the Ark had been captured by the Philistines, he fell over and died. He had spent his life trying to serve the Lord as a high priest, but the very first prophetic word given to Samuel was one of the most frightening rebukes given in the Scriptures—and it was directed to Eli!

> *For I have told him that I am about to judge his house forever for the iniquity which he knew, because his sons brought a curse on themselves and he did not rebuke them.*
>
> *Therefore I have sworn to the house of Eli that the iniquity of Eli's house shall not be atoned for by sacrifice or offering forever.*
>
> 1 Samuel 3:13-14

Eli's zeal for the Lord was based on sacrifices and offerings intended to compensate for his irresponsibility as a father. Guilt can spur us on to great zeal for the Lord and our sacrifices and offerings become an attempt to atone for our failures. This is an affront to the cross, which alone can atone for our guilt. Such zeal will never be acceptable to the Lord, even if we could make sacrifices forever.

We should note here that the Lord never said that Eli's sin couldn't be forgiven. He said that Eli's attempts to atone for sin *by sacrifice and offering* would never succeed. There are multitudes of men and women whose zeal for the Lord is likewise based on an attempt to atone for sin, failure, or irresponsibility in other areas of their lives. But all the sacrifices in the world will not atone for even our smallest failure. To even make such an attempt is an insult to the cross of Jesus, which is the only acceptable sacrifice to the Father for sin.

Attempting to gain God's approval by our own sacrifice opens the door wide for a religious spirit, because such service is not based on the blood of Jesus, but on an attempt to make our own atonement for sin. This does not mean we should not do things to please the Lord; it means our motive for pleasing the Lord is for His joy, not for our acceptance. One is God-centered; the other is self-centered. And this is self-centeredness of the most destructive kind—an attempt to circumvent the cross.

It is also noteworthy that one of the sins of Eli's sons was that they "...despised the offering of the Lord" (1 Sam. 2:17). They appropriated for their own selfish use the sacrifices and offerings brought to the Lord. Those who are gripped by this form of a religious spirit will often be the most zealous to preach the cross, but herein lies the perversion: It emphasizes *their* cross more than the cross of Jesus. Their real delight is more in self-abasement than in the cross of Christ, which alone makes us righteous and acceptable to God.

THE FOUNDATION OF PRIDE

Idealism is one of the most deceptive and destructive disguises of the religious spirit. Idealism is of human origin and is a form of humanism. Although it has the appearance of seeking only the highest standards and the preservation of God's glory, idealism is possibly the most deadly enemy of true revelation and true grace. It is deadly because it does not allow for growing up into grace and wisdom, rather it attacks and destroys the foundation of those who are in pursuit of God's glory, but are not yet there.

Idealism imposes on others standards that are beyond what God has required or given the grace for at that time. For example, men controlled by this kind of religious spirit may condemn those who are not praying two hours a day as they are. The truth is, it may be God's will for us to be praying that much, but how we get there is crucial. The grace of God may first call us to pray just ten minutes a day. Then, as we become so blessed by His presence, we will not want to quit after ten minutes but instead spend more and more time with Him until we pray for an hour, then two. When we are eventually praying two hours a day, it will be because of our love for prayer and the presence of the Lord, not out of fear or pride.

A person with a religious spirit based on idealism will usually seek the perfect church, and will refuse to be a part of anything less. Those led by the Holy Spirit may also have high hopes for a church, but will still be able to give themselves in service to even some of the most lowly works, in order to help those works grow in vision and maturity. The Holy Spirit is called "the Helper" (Jn. 14:26), and those who are truly led by the Spirit will always be looking for ways to help, not to stand aloof and criticize.

When a religious spirit is founded upon pride, it is evidenced by *perfectionism*. The perfectionist sees everything as black or white. This develops into extremes, requiring that every person and every teaching be judged as either 100 percent right or 100 percent wrong. This is a standard with which only Jesus could comply. It will lead to a serious delusion when we impose it on ourselves or others. True grace imparts a truth that sets people free, showing them the way out of their sin, and beckoning them to higher levels of spiritual maturity.

One with a religious spirit can usually point to problems with great accuracy, but seldom has solutions, except to tear down what has already been built. This is the strategy of the enemy to nullify progress that is being made and to sow discouragement that will limit future progress. This produces the mentality that if we cannot go straight to the top of the mountain, we should not climb at all, but just "die to self." This is a death that God has not required and it is a perversion of the exhortation for us to take up our crosses daily.

The perfectionist both imposes and tries to live by standards that stifle true maturity and growth. The grace of God will lead us up the mountain step-by-step. The Lord does not condemn us because we may trip a few times while trying to climb. He graciously picks us up with the encouragement that we can make it. We must have a vision of making it to the top, and should never condemn ourselves for not being there yet, *as long as we are still climbing.*

James said, "...we all stumble in many ways..." (Jas. 3:2). If we had to wait until we were perfect before we could minister, no one would ever qualify for the ministry. Even though perfect obedience and understanding should always be our goal, such will never be found within ourselves, but only as we come to perfectly abide in the Perfect One.

Because "now we see through a glass, darkly" (1 Cor. 13:12 KJV), or in part, we must always be open to greater accuracy in our beliefs and teachings. One of the greatest delusions of all is that we are already complete in our understanding, or 100 percent accurate in our perceptions or actions. Those with a religious spirit will usually claim to be open to more understanding, but most of the time this is done to convince *everyone else* to be open to what they teach, while they remain steadfastly closed to others.

Jesus blessed Peter and turned the keys of the kingdom over to him just before He had to rebuke him by calling him "satan" (see Mt. 16:23). Right after this greatest of blessings, the enemy deceived him, yet the Lord did not take the keys away from Peter! In fact, Jesus knew when He gave the keys to Peter that he would soon deny even knowing Him.

Many years after Peter used the keys to open the door of faith for both the Jews and Gentiles, "the least of the apostles," Paul, had to rebuke him publicly because of his hypocrisy (see 1 Cor. 15:9, Gal. 2:11-14). Even so, Peter was promised that he would sit on one of the twelve thrones judging the twelve tribes of Israel (see Mt. 19:28). The Lord has proven that He will commission and use men long before most of us would, and when He calls us, He already knows all the mistakes that we will make.

It seems that the Lord's leadership style was to provide a place where His followers could make mistakes and learn from them. If we require our children to be perfectly mature while they are still children, it stifles their growth and maturity. The same is true in the Church. We must correct mistakes, because that is how we learn, but it must be a correction that encourages and frees, not one that condemns and crushes initiative.

THE DEADLY COMBINATION

One of the most powerful and deceptive forms of the religious spirit is built upon the foundations of both fear and pride. Those who are bound in this way go through periods of deep anguish and remorse at their failures, but this false repentance results only in more self-abasement and further attempts to make sacrifices that will appease the Lord. Those bound by this religious spirit then often flip to the other side, where they become so convinced that they are superior to other Christians or other groups that they become unteachable and unable to receive reproof. The foundation that they stand on at any given time will be dictated more by external pressure than by true conviction.

Such a religious spirit is so slippery that it will wiggle out of almost any attempt to confront it. If you address the pride, the fears and insecurities will rise up to attract sympathy. If you confront the fear, it will then change into religious pride masquerading as faith. This type of spirit will drive individuals or congregations to such extremes that they will inevitably disintegrate.

THE COUNTERFEIT GIFT OF DISCERNMENT

A religious spirit will usually give a counterfeit gift of discernment of spirits that is motivated by suspicion and fear. This counterfeit gift thrives on seeing what is wrong with others rather than seeing what God is doing so we can help them along. Using this type of discernment, a religious spirit can cause some of its greatest damage to the Church. Its ministry will almost always leave more damage and division than healing, reconciliation, and building. Its wisdom is rooted in the Tree of the Knowledge of Good and Evil, and though the truth may be accurate, it is ministered in a spirit that kills.

Suspicion is rooted in such things as rejection, territorial preservation, or general insecurity. The true gift of discernment can only function through love. Any motive other than love will distort spiritual perception. Whenever someone submits a judgment or criticism about another person or group, we should disregard it unless we know that the one bringing it truly loves that person or group, and has an "investment" of service to them.

SUMMARY

As you have probably already deduced, all evil spiritual strongholds have similar characteristics. Their tactics and functions often overlap to become a web that captures and then holds its prey. Of all the fortresses of deception that the enemy has built among men, the religious spirit has been the most deceptive and deadly, because it comes as a pretense of righteousness and goodness.

Even though this spirit comes with a pretense for righteousness, it is discerned by how it always has us looking at ourselves, trying to measure ourselves against standards, comparing ourselves to others, and consequently distracting us from the glory of God that transforms us. The religious spirit is therefore the most concentrated fruit from the Tree of the Knowledge of Good and Evil. The "good" side of this tree is just as deadly as the evil—the fruit of the religious spirit will always be spiritual death. In the next chapters we will study other manifestations of this spirit, how it gains entry into our lives, and how we can be free from it.

Chapter Fourteen

Angels of Light

When Paul warned the Corinthians about those who ministered in a religious spirit, which sought to bring a yoke of legalism upon the young Church, he explained that:

> *For such men are false apostles, deceitful workers, disguising themselves as apostles of Christ.*
>
> *No wonder, for even Satan disguises himself as an angel of light.*
>
> *Therefore it is not surprising if his servants also disguise themselves as servants of righteousness....*
>
> 2 Corinthians 11:13-15

In this text Paul was specifically talking about those from among the Jews who were seeking to bring the Gentile converts under the yoke of the Law of Moses. This was the first and most deadly heresy to impose itself on the young Church. It has been compared to the temptation of Eve, as the Church is called to be the Bride of Christ, the "last Adam"; and this was a second attempt by the devil to seduce the Bride to partake of the Tree of Knowledge again. It succeeded with many during that time.

Paul and the other apostles wrote large portions of the New Testament to combat this deception, warning believers that the result of turning back to the Law of Moses would actually sever them from Christ (see Gal. 5:4). It is noteworthy that this same heresy is arising again among some Messianic groups.

The phrase often used by the apostles in the first century was that there were "false apostles," "angels of light," etc. Satan's most deceptive and deadly disguise is to come as a servant of righteousness, using truths for the purpose of destruction. The devil is quite skillful at quoting Scripture and using wisdom, but it is the wisdom of the Tree of Knowledge— wisdom that kills.

Because Paul was the champion of grace and the pure message of the gospel, the later form of this heresy most especially undermines his New Testament letters, while at the same time persuading different people groups that they are the descendants of ten "lost tribes of Israel." This false doctrine urges people to base their identity on the flesh instead of by the Spirit through being born again into Christ. This sounds ridiculous to those who are well-grounded in the New Covenant, but tragically, many Christians are not well-grounded. This heresy effectively severs many from a true relationship to Jesus through the cross. If it has not yet attacked your church, it almost certainly will.

This new form of the original heresy to seduce the Church into turning to the Law of Moses for righteousness is but one form in which these "angels of light" come. All who are empowered by a religious spirit will have a tendency to get us focused on what is wrong with ourselves or the Church, rather than for what is right. Although this spirit usually comes in the guise of protecting the sheep, the truth, or the Lord's glory, it is an evil, critical spirit that will always end up causing division and destruction.

Criticism has an appearance of wisdom, but it is pride in one of its most base forms. When we criticize someone, we are in effect declaring ourselves to be better than them. We may be better than others in some areas, but if we are, it is only by grace. Believers who recognize the true grace of God never look for ways to put others down, but rather find ways to build them up. As an old proverb declares, "Any jackass can kick a barn down, but it requires a skillful carpenter to build one."

THE RELIGIOUS SPIRIT AND MURDER

When Adam and Eve chose to live by the Knowledge of Good and Evil, they were partaking of the religious spirit. The first result of this was self-centeredness—they started looking at themselves. The first child born to them after partaking of this fruit was Cain, who is the first biblical model of a man controlled by the religious spirit.

"...Cain was a tiller of the ground" (Gen. 4:2), or earthly-minded. The religious spirit will always seek to keep us focused on the earthly realm rather than the heavenly realm. This "seed of Cain" judges by what is seen, and cannot understand those who "...endured, as seeing Him who is unseen" (Heb. 11:27).

In Revelation 13:11, we see the second beast "coming up *out of the earth.*" This is because the spiritual seed of Cain are tillers of the ground. This earthly-mindedness has produced one of the most evil beasts the world will ever know.

Cain also tried to make an offering to the Lord from his own labors. God rejected that sacrifice, but accepted Abel's sacrifice of blood. The fruit of our labors will never be an acceptable offering to the Lord. This was a statement from the

145

beginning that God would only accept the blood of the Lamb. Instead of receiving this correction and repenting, Cain became jealous of his brother and killed him. Those who attempt to live by their own works will often become enraged at those who take their stand on the righteousness of the Lamb.

That is precisely why Saul of Tarsus, the Pharisee of Pharisees, was so enraged against Christians. They represented the greatest threat to that on which the Pharisees had built their whole lives. Because of this, the Pharisees could not endure the very existence of the Christians. Religions that are based on works will easily become violent. This includes "Christian" sects where a doctrine of works has supplanted the cross of Christ.

The Lord said that if a man hates his brother he is guilty of murder (see Mt. 5:21-22). Those who are driven by religious spirits may well try to destroy people by means other than the physical taking of their lives. Many of the onslaughts of slander instigated against churches and ministries are the ragings of this same religious spirit that caused Cain to slay his brother.

THE TEST OF A TRUE MESSENGER

In Ezekiel 37 the prophet was taken to a valley full of dry bones and asked if the bones could live. The Lord then commanded him to "prophesy to the bones." As he prophesied they came together, came to life, and then became a great army.

This is an important test that every true ministry must pass. The true prophet can see a great army in even the driest of bones. He will prophesy life to those bones until they come to life and then become an army. A false prophet with a religious spirit will do little more than just tell the bones how dry they are, heaping discouragement and condemnation on them, while imparting no life or power to overcome their circumstances.

Apostles and prophets are given authority to build up and tear down, but we have no right to tear down if we have not first built up. We should give no one the authority to bring correction to the people under our care unless they first have a history of providing spiritual nourishment and building people up. Some may say that such a policy would eliminate the ministry of the prophets altogether, but I say that so-called "prophets" who do not have a heart to build people up *should be* eliminated from ministry. Jude said they are grumblers, fault finders who are "hidden reefs in your love feasts" (see Jude 12-16).

Even so, as we can see from Eli's tragic example, woe to the shepherds who feed and care for the sheep, but fail to *correct* them. The true grace of God is found between the extremes of unrighteous faultfinding and unsanctified mercy (approving of things that God condemns). Either extreme can be the result of a religious spirit.

CHAPTER FIFTEEN

OTHER MASKS OF THE RELIGIOUS SPIRIT

WHAT IS POPULARLY CALLED the "Jezebel spirit" is a form of the religious spirit. Just as Jezebel was the ambitious and manipulative wife of King Ahab—a weak leader who allowed her to dictate policy in his kingdom—the Jezebel spirit will usually be found supplanting weak leadership. The Jezebel spirit usually gains its dominion by making political alliances and often uses a deceptively humble and submissive demeanor in order to manipulate. However, once this spirit gains authority, it will usually manifest a strong control spirit and shameless presumption. Despite its name, this spiritual problem is not limited to women.

Jezebel "calls herself a prophetess" (Rev. 2:20). This is often one of the telltale signs of false prophets who are operating in a religious spirit—they are preoccupied with their own recognition. To the degree that self-seeking and the need for recognition abides within us, our ministry will be corrupted.

Those who are easily offended because they are not given an important title or position should never be accepted by that title or given that position! The key difference between those motivated by a desire for recognition and those motivated by love for the Lord is the difference between the false prophet and the true. As we read in John 7:17-18, those who seek their own recognition speak from themselves, but those who are seeking the recognition of the One who sent them are true.

Demanding recognition for herself, Jezebel serves as the enemy of the true prophetic ministry. Jezebel was the greatest enemy of one of the Old Covenant's most powerful prophets, Elijah, whose ministry especially typified preparing the way for the Lord. The Jezebel spirit is one of the most potent forms of the religious spirit, which seeks to keep the Church and the world from being prepared for the return of the Lord.

The Jezebel spirit especially attacks the prophetic ministry because that ministry has an important place in preparing the way for the Lord. That is why John the Baptist was persecuted by a personification of Jezebel, in the wife of Herod. The prophetic ministry is the primary vehicle through which the Lord gives timely, strategic direction to His people. Jezebel knows that removing the true prophets will make the people vulnerable to her false prophets, always resulting in idolatry and spiritual adultery.

When there is a void of hearing the true voice of the Lord, the people will be much more susceptible to the deceptions of the enemy. This is why Jesus called the religious leaders of His own day "blind guides" (see Mt. 23:16). These men, who knew the messianic prophecies better than anyone else in the world, looked into the face of the One who perfectly fulfilled those prophecies and thought that He was sent from Beelzebub.

Jezebel's prophets of Baal were also given to sacrifice, even to the point of cutting and flailing themselves while seeking the manifestation of their god. A primary strategy of the religious spirit is to get the church devoted to "sacrifice" in a way that perverts the command for us to take up our crosses daily. This perversion will have us putting more faith in our sacrifices than in the Lord's sacrifice. It will also use sacrifices and offerings to pressure God to manifest Himself. This is a form of the terrible delusion that we can somehow purchase the grace and presence of God with our good works.

THE ROOT OF SELF-RIGHTEOUSNESS

We do not crucify ourselves for the sake of righteousness, purification, spiritual maturity, or to get the Lord to manifest Himself; this is nothing more than conjuring. We are "crucified with Christ" (Gal. 2:20). If we "crucify ourselves," the only result is self-righteousness—which is pride in one of its most base forms. This pride is deceptive, because it gives the appearance of wisdom and righteousness, of which the apostle Paul warned:

> Let no one keep defrauding you of your prize by delighting in self-abasement and the worship of the angels, taking his stand on visions he has seen, inflated without cause by his fleshly mind,
>
> and not holding fast to the head, from whom the entire body, being supplied and held together by the joints and ligaments, grows with a growth which is from God.
>
> If you have died with Christ to the elementary principles of the world, why, as if you were living in the world, do you submit yourself to decrees, such as,

"Do not handle, do not taste, do not touch!"

(which all refer to things destined to perish with the using)—in accordance with the commandments and teachings of men?

These are matters which have, to be sure, the appearance of wisdom in self-made religion and self-abasement and severe treatment of the body, but are of no value against fleshly indulgence.

Colossians 2:18-23

The religious spirit will make us feel very good about our spiritual condition as long as it is self-centered and self-seeking. Pride feels good; it can even be exhilarating. But it keeps all of our attention on how well we are doing and on how we stand compared to others—not on the glory of God. Consequently we put our confidence in discipline and personal sacrifice rather than in the Lord and His sacrifice.

Of course, discipline and a commitment to self-sacrifice are essential qualities for every believer to have. But it is the motivation behind them that determines whether we are being driven by a religious spirit or by the Holy Spirit. A religious spirit motivates through fear and guilt, or through pride and ambition. The motivation of the Holy Spirit is love for the Son of God.

Delighting in self-abasement is a sure symptom of the religious spirit. This does not mean we can neglect to discipline ourselves, fast, or buffet our bodies as Paul did. However, the problem comes when we take a perverse delight in this, rather than delighting in the Son of God.

DECEPTIVE REVELATION

Colossians 2:18-19 indicates that a person with a religious spirit will tend to delight in self-abasement and will often be given to worshiping angels or taking improper stands on visions he has seen. A religious spirit wants us to worship anything or anyone but Jesus. The same spirit that is given to worshiping angels will also be prone to excessively exalting people.

We must beware of anyone who unduly exalts angels or men and women of God, or anyone who uses the visions he has received in order to gain improper influence in the Church. God does not give us revelations so that people will respect us more, or to prove our ministries. The fruit of true revelation will be humility, not pride.

Of course, the Scriptures teach that Christians do have prophetic experiences, and we are told in Acts 2:17 that they will increase in the last days. Jesus also warned that in the last days there would be many false prophets (see Mt. 24:11). Prophetic revelation that is truly from God is crucial to the Body of Christ. The enemy knows this very well, which is why he will raise up many false prophets. But they can be easily discerned. As Paul warned the Colossians, the danger does not come from those who are *having* prophetic revelations, but from those who have been *inflated* by them.

A religious spirit will always feed our fear or pride, whereas genuine spiritual maturity will always lead to increasing humility. This progression of humility is wonderfully demonstrated in the life of Paul the apostle. In his letter to the Galatians, estimated to have been written in A.D. 56, he declared that when he visited the original apostles in Jerusalem, they "...contributed nothing to me" (Gal. 2:6). He was by this declaring that he had as much as they did.

In Paul's first letter to the Corinthians, written about six years later, he called himself the "least of the apostles" (1 Cor. 15:9). In Ephesians 3:8, written in about A.D. 61, he declared himself to be the "the very least of all saints." When writing to Timothy in approximately A.D. 65, Paul declared himself to be the foremost of all sinners (see 1 Tim. 1:15), adding that he had found mercy. *A true revelation of God's mercy is a great antidote for the religious spirit.*

It is clear by these Scriptures that the great apostle was not completely free of pride in the first years of his ministry. Which of us can claim to be free of it either? However, we are all hopefully growing in grace and, therefore, humility.

Young apostles may exude a lot of pride, but they can still be true apostles. The key here is in which direction we are heading. Are we being puffed up by our revelations, our commissions, or our accomplishments? Or are we growing in grace and humility?

The Martyr Syndrome

When combined with the religious spirit, the martyr syndrome is one of the ultimate and most deadly delusions. To be a true martyr for the faith and literally lose our lives for the sake of Christ is one of the greatest honors that we can receive in this life. Yet when this is perverted, it is a most tragic form of deception.

When a religious spirit is combined with the martyr syndrome it is almost impossible for that person to be delivered from the deception that he is "suffering for the gospel." At this point, any rejection or correction received from others is perceived as the price he must pay to "stand for the truth." This warped perspective will drive him even further from the truth and any possibility of correction.

The martyr syndrome can also be a manifestation of the spirit of suicide. It is sometimes easier to "die for the Lord"

than it is to live for Him. Those who have a perverted understanding of the cross glory more in death than they do in life.
They fail to see that the point of the cross is the resurrection,
not the grave.

SELF-HELP PSYCHOLOGY

There is a "self-help psychology" movement that is attempting to replace the power of the cross in the Church.
Humanistically-based psychology is what Paul calls "a different
gospel" (see 2 Cor. 11:4); it is an enemy of the cross, and is
another form of the religious spirit. Paul also warned:

*As you, therefore, have received Christ Jesus the Lord, so
walk in Him,*

*having been firmly rooted and now being built up in Him
and established in your faith, just as you were instructed,
and overflowing with gratitude.*

*See to it that no one takes you captive through philosophy
and empty deception, according to the tradition of men,
according to the elementary principles of the world, rather
than according to Christ.*

Colossians 2:6-8

We all need "inner healing" to some degree, but much of
what is being called inner healing is nothing more than digging
up the "old man" and trying to get him healed. The answer to
these deep wounds is not a procedure or a formula, but simple
forgiveness. When we go to the cross and find forgiveness and
true acceptance based on the blood of Jesus, we will find a
perfect love able to cast out all our fears and wash away all
bitterness and resentment.

This seems too simple, and that is why Paul said: "...I am afraid, lest as the serpent deceived Eve by his craftiness, your minds will be led astray from the simplicity and purity of devotion to Christ" (2 Cor. 11:3). Salvation is simple. Deliverance is simple. Yet one of the enemy's major strategies is diluting the power of the gospel by having us add to it, which is how Eve was deceived. We add to it because we do not think it is acceptable unless it somehow seems brilliant or abstract. That is precisely why we must become like children to enter the Kingdom.

The Lord commanded the man and woman not to eat from the Tree of the Knowledge of Good and Evil because they would die. When the serpent asked about this command, Eve replied that they could not eat from the tree "*or touch it*" (see Gen. 3:3). However, the Lord had not said anything about refraining from touching the tree.

Adding to God's commandments is just as destructive as taking away from them. Anyone who thinks that he can so flippantly add to the Word of God does not respect it enough to keep it when the testing comes. If satan can get us to either add or subtract from the Word, then he knows our fall is imminent, just as it was for Eve.

Although there are many "Christian" philosophies and therapies that seem wise, most are in fact attempting to be substitutes for the Holy Spirit in our lives. Some people do need counseling, and there are outstanding Christian counselors who do lead people to the cross. But others are simply leading people into a black hole of self-centeredness that will consume them and try to suck in everyone else around them as well. In spite of the Christian terminology, this philosophy is an enemy of the cross of Christ.

Chapter Sixteen

The Warning Signs of a Religious Spirit

The following is a list of some of the more obvious warning signs of the religious spirit. As stated, almost everyone is battling the religious spirit at least to some degree, and everyone's fight is somewhat different. One may be dealing with all the issues listed below to a small degree, and yet be more free from the yoke of the religious spirit than one who has serious problems with just a couple of them.

Our goal is to be completely free of any influence from the religious spirit by being completely submitted to the Holy Spirit. Without complete submission to the Lord there is no way to be free from the religious spirit.

People with a religious spirit:

1. *Will often see their primary mission as the tearing down of whatever they believe is wrong.* Such a person's ministry will result more in division and destruction than in lasting works that bear fruit for the Kingdom.

2. *Will be unable to accept a rebuke, especially from those they judge to be less spiritual than themselves.* Think back on how you responded the last few times someone tried to correct you.

3. *Will have a philosophy that, "I will not listen to people, but only to God."* Since God frequently speaks through people this is an obvious delusion, revealing serious spiritual pride.

4. *Will be inclined to see more of what is wrong than what is right with other people, other churches, etc.* From the valley John saw Babylon, but when he was carried to a high mountain, he saw the New Jerusalem (see Rev. 21:10). If we are seeing only Babylon, it is because of our perspective. Those who are in a place of true vision will have their attention on what God is doing, not men.

5. *Will be subject to an overwhelming feeling of guilt that they can never measure up to the Lord's standards.* Guilt is a root of the religious spirit because it causes us to base our relationship with Him on our performance rather than on the cross. Jesus has already measured up for us. He is the completed work that the Father is seeking to accomplish within us. Our whole goal in life should be simply to abide in Him.

6. *Will keep score on their spiritual life.* This includes feeling better about ourselves because we go to more meetings, read our Bibles more, do more things for the Lord, etc. These are all noble endeavors, but the true measure of spiritual maturity is getting closer to the Lord.

7. *Will believe that they have been appointed to fix everyone else.* These persons become the self-appointed watchmen or sheriffs in God's Kingdom. They are seldom involved in building, but serve only to keep the Church in a state of annoyance and agitation, if not causing serious divisions.

8. *Will have a leadership style that is bossy, overbearing, and intolerant of the weakness or failure of others.* James said: "But the wisdom from above is first pure, then peaceable, gentle, reasonable, full of mercy and good fruits, unwavering, without hypocrisy. And the seed whose fruit is righteousness is sown in peace by those who make peace" (Jas. 3:17-18).

9. *Will have a sense that they are closer to God than other people, or that their lives or ministries are more pleasing to Him.* This is a symptom of the profound delusion that we draw closer to God because of who we are, rather than through Jesus.

10. *Will take pride in their spiritual maturity and discipline, especially as compared to others.* True spiritual maturity involves growing up into Christ. When we begin to compare ourselves to others, it is obvious that we have lost sight of the true goal—Jesus.

11. *Will believe that they are on the "cutting edge" of what God is doing.* This includes thinking that we are involved in the most important thing that God is doing.

12. *Will have a mechanical prayer life.* When we start feeling relief that our prayer time is over or that we have finally prayed through our prayer list, we should consider our condition. We will never feel relief when our conversations are over with the One we love.

13. *Will do things in order to be noticed by people.* This is a symptom of the idolatry of fearing people more than we fear God, which results in a religion that serves men instead of God.

14. *Will be overly repulsed by emotionalism.* When people who are subject to a religious spirit encounter the true life of God, it will usually appear to them to be excessive, emotional, and carnal. True passion for God is often emotional and demonstrative,

such as David exemplified when he brought the ark of God into Jerusalem (see 2 Sam. 6:14-16).

15. *Will use emotionalism as a substitute for the work of the Holy Spirit.* This seems contradictory to the previous point, but the religious spirit will often take contradictory positions in its drive for self-preservation and exaltation. This use of emotionalism will include such things as requiring weeping and wailing as evidence of repentance, or "falling under the power" as evidence that one has been touched by God. Both of these can be evidences of the true work of the Holy Spirit, but when we *require* these manifestations we are beginning to move in another spirit.

At Jonathan Edwards' meetings during the First Great Awakening, some of the toughest, most rebellious men would fall to the ground and stay there for up to 24 hours. They got up changed, however, and such strange manifestations of the Holy Spirit fueled the Great Awakenings. Even so, Edwards stated that people faking the manifestations did more to bring an end to the Great Awakening than did the enemies of the revival!

16. *Will be encouraged when their ministries look better than others.* We could also include in this being discouraged when it seems that others are looking better or growing faster than they are.

17. *Will glory more in what God did in the past than in what He is doing in the present.* God has not changed—He is the same yesterday, today, and forever. The veil has been removed, and we can be as close to God today as anyone ever has been in the past. A religious spirit will always seek to focus our attention on works and on making comparisons, rather than on simply drawing closer to the Lord.

18. *Will tend to be suspicious of, or opposed to, new movements, churches, etc.* This is an obvious symptom of jealousy, a primary fruit of the religious spirit, or the pride that asserts that God would not do anything new without doing it through us. Of course, those with such a mentality are seldom used by the Lord to birth new works.

19. *Will tend to reject spiritual manifestations that they do not understand.* This is a symptom of the pride and arrogance of presuming our opinions are the same as God's. True humility keeps us teachable and open, patiently waiting for fruit before making judgments. True discernment enables us to look for and hope for the best, not the worst. For this reason, we are exhorted to "...examine everything carefully; hold fast to that which is good," not what is bad (1 Thess. 5:21).

20. *Will overreact to carnality in the Church.* The truth is, there is probably far more carnality in the Church, and a lot less of the Holy Spirit, than even the most critical person has guessed. It is important that we learn to discern between them in order to be delivered from our carnality and grow in our submission to the Holy Spirit. But the critical person will annihilate those who may still be 60 percent carnal, but were 95 percent carnal last year. Instead, we need to recognize that people are making progress and do what we can to help them along the way.

21. *Will overreact to immaturity in the Church.* There is an immaturity that is acceptable to the Lord. My two-year-old is immature when compared to my nine-year-old, but that is to be expected; and in fact, he may be very mature for a two-year-old. The idealistic religious spirit only sees the immaturity, without considering the other important factors.

22. *Will be overly prone to view supernatural manifestations as evidence of God's approval.* This is just another form of keeping score and comparing ourselves with others. Some of Jesus' greatest miracles, such as walking on water, were seen by only a few. His works were done to glorify the Father, not Himself. Those who use the evidence of miracles to promote and build their own ministries and reputations have made a serious departure from the path of life.

23. *Will be unable to join anything that they do not deem perfect or nearly perfect.* The Lord joined, and even gave His life for the fallen human race. Such is the nature of those who abide in Him.

24. *Will be overly paranoid of the religious spirit.* We do not get free of something by fearing it, but by overcoming it with faith in Christ Jesus.

25. *Will have the tendency to glory in anything but the cross of Jesus, what He has accomplished, and who He is.* If we are building our lives, ministries, or churches on anything else, we are building on a shaky foundation that will not stand.

CHECK YOURSELF

While reading through this list, if you thought continually of how it relates to someone else, but really could not see how much it applies to you, you may have the biggest problem of all. Those with a religious spirit usually have such a "log in their own eye" that they cannot see their own problems. Again, as Paul exhorted us: "Test yourselves to see if you are in the faith..." (2 Cor. 13:5). First, He did not say to "test your neighbor" or to "test your pastor," but to "test *yourselves.*" Using this test to measure others can be a symptom that we have a serious problem.

If this list has given you illumination about problems in another person, church, or ministry, be sure that you respond in the Holy Spirit, heeding Paul's warning to the Galatians:

Brethren, even if anyone is caught in any trespass, you who are spiritual, restore such a one in a spirit of gentleness; each one looking to yourself, lest you too be tempted.

Galatians 6:1

It is the tendency of a religious spirit to separate us from other believers. Therefore, the tendency to cut off fellowship with anyone because they have these problems is an indication that we have a problem ourselves. Love helps. The Holy Spirit is called "the Helper" because that is His nature. If we are following the Holy Spirit, helping will always be our tendency when someone else has problems.

CHAPTER SEVENTEEN

TEN THINGS WE CAN DO TO GET FREE OF THE RELIGIOUS SPIRIT

I HAVE BEEN SOMEWHAT RETICENT to try to formulate this list for obvious reasons. Those who are bound by a religious spirit may tend to interpret this list in a manner that promotes more religious activity in place of true intimacy with the Lord. However, I trust that if you have the humility to read this, the Lord will give you His grace to use this list properly: as suggested guidelines to help us draw closer to Him.

1. *Develop a secret relationship with the Lord.* The Lord warned His disciples not to be like the Pharisees who did their works to be noticed by men, but to do their works in secret before the Father. In this way we begin to put our hope and trust in our relationship to Him, not men. There is no greater security than to know that we are known by God. As the Lord warned, "How can you believe, when you receive glory one from another and you do not seek the glory that is from the

one and only God?" (Jn. 5:44) Seeking glory, or recognition, from men is probably the most destructive thing that we can do to true faith.

2. *Pray that the same love with which the Father loved the Son would be in you.* The Lord Jesus Himself prayed for the same love with which the Father loved Him to be in us (see Jn. 17:26). We know that this prayer of the Son of God, who was in perfect harmony with the Father, will be answered. But we have not because we ask not. When this love replaces religious duty, our good works will greatly exceed what they would be without it.

3. *"Study to show thyself approved unto God...[not men]"* (2 Tim. 2:15 KJV). When we study the Word of God in order to demonstrate our knowledge before men, or to prove our position before men, we have departed from the Spirit of Truth that leads to truth. The Spirit of Truth came to reveal Jesus, not us. We must study His Word in order to seek Him, and to do what is approved of Him, not men. As the Lord warned the Pharisees, "...You are those who justify yourselves in the sight of men, but God knows your hearts; for that which is highly esteemed among men is detestable in the sight of God" (Lk. 16:15). If we are motivated to do the things that are highly esteemed of men or to justify ourselves before men, we will be doing that which is detestable in God's sight.

4. *Spend quality time alone with the Lord each day.* Endeavor, as much as it is possible, to increase this time to the place where you spend more time alone with the Lord than with any other individual. When we are spending time with Him continually, we will not be so prone to the guilt that drives us to start measuring our spiritual lives by our works.

5. *Seek to hear the voice of the Lord every day.* The Lord's sheep know His voice (see Jn. 10:27). They know His voice because they

spend time with Him. If a good earthly parent seeks to spend some quality time with their children each day, how much more does the Lord seek to spend quality time with us? The quality of the time can be measured by the quality of the communication. The Lord really does want to speak to all of us each day. If we would refuse to go to bed until we have heard from Him in some meaningful way, our lives would quickly change. The most important thing that we can do each day is to spend time with Him and hear from Him. But do not just seek to hear the words of the Lord, but the Word Himself.

6. *Ask the Lord to give you the love for your neighbors that He has for them.* Only then will our witness and our ministry to them be pure. But we must always endeavor to love the Lord first and foremost. If we love the Lord more than we do our children, or our neighbors, we will love them more than we would otherwise.

7. *Seek to turn your criticisms into intercession.* Your first response to seeing something wrong with someone else should be to pray for them, asking for grace on their behalf. If someone especially irritates you, endeavor to pray for them even more. If you make an investment in them in prayer, "...where your treasure is, there your heart will be also" (Mt. 6:21), you will start to genuinely love them. True spiritual authority is founded on love; so if you love them enough, the Lord may be able to trust you with the ministry of truth that will set them free. Some of the greatest spiritual victories that are counted in Heaven are the ones that turn enemies into friends, and turn those who dwell in darkness into children of the light. This must always be our goal.

8. *Continually ask the Lord to see His glory.* It is by seeing His glory with an unveiled face that we are changed into His same

image (see 2 Cor. 3:18). Understanding doctrine is important, but until we see His glory, it remains only doctrine. When we behold Him the doctrine will become our nature. It is not by believing in our minds, but in our hearts, that results in righteousness.

9. *Keep as one of your highest goals to manifest the sweet aroma of the knowledge of God in every place.* Like Moses, ask the Lord not to send you anywhere that His manifest presence is not going to go with you. We should only want to be where He is. And we should always behave as is befitting in the presence of the King.

10. *When you have failed to do any of the things listed above properly, ask forgiveness, "...forgetting those things which are behind...press toward the mark for the prize of the high calling of God in Christ Jesus"* (Phil. 3:13-14 KJV).

CONCLUSION

Basically, the religious spirit seeks to replace the Holy Spirit as the source of spiritual life. It does this by seeking to replace true repentance, which leads to grace, with a repentance based on our performance. The effect is to replace true humility with pride.

True religion is based on loving the Lord and then loving our neighbors. True religion will promote discipline and obedience founded on love for the Lord rather than the need or desire for recognition or acceptance. The wife who keeps herself in shape because she loves her husband will be easily distinguished from the one who does it because of her own ego. The former will carry her beauty with grace and dignity; the latter may be physically appealing, but it will be a seductive appeal that is a perversion of true love.

The religious spirit is basically a manifestation of the "good" side of the Tree of the Knowledge of Good and Evil. When Adam and Eve ate of that tree in the Garden, the first result was that they looked at themselves. Self-centeredness is the poison that made that fruit deadly, and it is still the most deadly poison the serpent seeks to give us. In contrast with the religious spirit—which causes us to focus our attention on ourselves and base our concept of the Christian life on performance—the Holy Spirit will always lead us into a life that is Christ-centered.

The Holy Spirit produces fruit by joining us to the Lord and applying the work He accomplished for us on the cross: "For the word of the cross is to those who are perishing foolishness, but to us who are being saved it is the power of God" (1 Cor. 1:18). However, we must understand that this is the cross of Christ, not our own cross. We are called to deny ourselves and take up our crosses daily, but we are not to glory in self-abasement or try to live by the virtue of our own sacrifices. Rather, we are to glory in what Jesus accomplished and the sacrifice that *He* made (see Phil. 3:3).

We have our standing before God solely on the basis of the cross of Christ. Our ability to come boldly before the throne of God has nothing to do with whether we have had a good or bad day, or how properly we have performed all of our religious duties. Our acceptance before God and our ability to come into His presence is based on one thing only—the sacrifice that Jesus made for our justification.

His sacrifice does not negate the need for personal holiness, for as James asserted, "...faith, if it has no works, is dead..." (Jas. 2:17). If we are joined to Christ, we will not go on living in sin. However, we do not become free from sin in order to abide in Him, but by abiding in Him. Jesus is the Way, the Truth, and the Life. If He is not our Life, then we do not really know the Way or the Truth either. It is the religious spirit that tries to keep Christianity in the realm of the Way and the Truth, while keeping us from the essential union by which Jesus becomes our Life. True Christianity involves not just *what* we believe, but *Who* we believe.

True worship does not have as its purpose to see the Lord—rather, worship comes from having seen Him. When we see Him, we will worship. When we see His glory, we will no longer be captivated by our own positive or negative qualities— our souls will be captured by His beauty. When the Lamb enters, even the twenty-four elders will cast their crowns at His feet (see Rev. 4:10). That is the goal of true faith— to see Him, to abide in Him, and to reveal Him.

The world is becoming increasingly repulsed by religion. However, when Jesus is lifted up, all men will be drawn to Him (see Jn. 12:32). Because the whole creation was created through Him and for Him, we all have a Jesus-size hole in our soul. Nothing else will ever satisfy the longing of the human heart or bring us peace, except a genuine relationship with Christ Jesus.

When we are truly joined to Jesus, unstoppable living waters begin to flow out of our innermost beings. As more and more people are freed and this water begins to flow in them, it will become a great river of life in the midst of the earth. Those who drink from this river will never thirst again; they will have found satisfaction for the deepest yearning of the human soul. The more we get free of the religious spirit, the purer and clearer these waters will be.

WHERE DO WE GO FROM HERE?

THIS BOOK IS A BASIC STUDY of three strongholds. Hopefully, as you read, you were able to think of many other applications and manifestations of these evil powers. My goal was to lay a foundation of general knowledge upon which the Holy Spirit could build an even greater understanding. These "revelations" are arrows in your quiver. Use them wisely.

For information about the ministry of Rick Joyner and other books and materials that are available by him, you can call 1-800-542-0278 for a free catalog or visit the website at **www.morningstarministries.org.**

Also by
RICK JOYNER

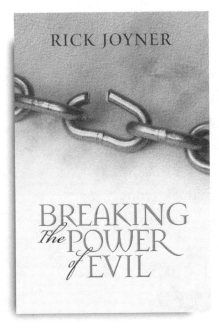

BREAKING THE POWER OF EVIL

The gates of hell are the entrances through which evil gains access to the world. Rick Joyner, author of the best-selling book *The Final Quest*, dramatically exposes the insidious cruelty of evil as manifested in jealousy, fear, spirit of poverty, spiritual authority, and religious spirits. *Breaking the Power of Evil* equips the Church with the tools necessary to first create a barrier to our world and then open a door into the heavenly realm. Joyner declares that the battle is one of territory—one that is a struggle for the human heart. It is in the heart where evil must be broken. With prophetic precision, Joyner carefully casts a prophetic light that will dispel the darkness as it enlightens the soul.

ISBN: 0-7684-2163-2

Additional copies of this book and other book titles from DESTINY IMAGE are available at your local bookstore.

For a complete list of our titles, visit us at www.destinyimage.com Send a request for a catalog to:

Destiny Image® Publishers, Inc.

P.O. Box 310
Shippensburg, PA 17257-0310

"Speaking to the Purposes of God for This Generation and for the Generations to Come"